DEFERRED FUTURE

DEFERRED FUTURE

Corporate and World Debt and Bankruptcy

_____Dan Dimancescu_____

Ballinger Publishing Company ● Cambridge, Massachusetts
A Subsidiary of Harper & Row, Publishers, Inc.

International Standard Book Number: 0-88410-360-9

Library of Congress Catalog Card Number: 83-15500

Printed in the United States of America

Library of Congress Cataloging in Publication Data

Dimancescu, Dan.
  Deferred future.

  Includes index.
    1. Debt. 2. Debts, External—Developing countries.
3. Bankruptcy. I. Title.
HG3701.D55 1983   336.3'435'091724   83-15500
ISBN 0-88410-360-9

CONTENTS

CONTENTS

Preface

MY INTEREST in debt and bankruptcy is due in part to my personal peripatetic encounters with debt. Having experienced the difficulties of running a corporation saddled with debt and under daily pressures from creditors, I can easily empathize with other individuals, corporations, and even nations experiencing similar pressure. There is nothing simple about indebtedness, for in it are wrapped immense emotional burdens, a seeming amorality of creditor interests, the coldness of juridical proceedings, and often, fickle standards of behavior. The joke, or lesson, about borrowing is that it is better to go for the huge loan than for the little one. The big loan, if defaulted on, gets the bank in trouble. It becomes "their" problem. The small loan, if defaulted on, gets you in trouble. It becomes "your" problem. From this lesson emerges a double standard. The big corporate borrower who defaults is excused with the respectful and forgiving aside: "Well he always took big risks! He'll make it next time." The small borrower who defaults and loses his shirt is offered the rebuke: "He's getting what he deserved! He should have known better."

Such standards are not unlike those evident in how we perceive Third World debt. Somehow it seems acceptable to bankers that Mexico and Brazil, who owe enormous amounts to foreign lenders, can rationalize the accumulation of debt on which they are now defaulting. Their debt—as large as it has become—is now the bankers' problem. The little economies, like Costa Rica, get whiplashed by their bankers. The lesson of borrowing was learned all too well by a few nations whose appetite for foreign capital was allowed to go uncontrolled. These habits have come now to threaten the stability of the entire world economy. Such behavior requires better understanding and calls for more rigor in determining appropriate levels of indebtedness—whether for nations, corporations, or individuals.

If such questions intrigued me as a stimulus for writing this book, I also owe part of the original idea to Richard Gerrity, a businessman and friend from Albany, New York. Gerrity, whose interest in buying and turning around bankrupt properties is more than a decade old, provided me with an intimate insight into the day-to-day operations of one of his own companies. The fragility of making failure turn to success quickly became evident, and the taxing personal commitment required by an entrepreneur such as Gerrity faced with bank debt, weekly employee payrolls, threatened law suits, and a need to sustain confidence with clients and suppliers impressed me greatly. This was hardly a task for the weak hearted. Gerrity's interest and support were important ingredients in leading this book to its completion.

The book's evolution is due also to the constant and enthusiastic involvement of Carol Franco, the senior editor of Ballinger Publishing Company. Sharing preliminary chapters with an editor is often done with trepidation because of the numerous problems that first drafts display. Carol always saw through to the substance and potential of the manuscript and continually offered encouragement. Additional help was provided by family and friends, whose readings of partially completed drafts proved invaluable. My wife Katherine who read drafts and shared in the enthusiasm of seeing them progress, and my daughter Katie who by the time the manuscript was finished was two years old and highly adept at creating wildly confusing patterns of letters—hhhhxMM****66....—on my Wang word processor. Dimitri Dimancescu, my brother, Anthony Phipps, and William Sahlman at the Harvard Business School were particularly generous with constructive suggestions. The writing of many chapters could not have been done without the meticulous and orderly gathering of voluminous background data and documentation by the staff of the Center for Strategy Research—in particular, Mary Ann Burns and the firm's founder, Christopher Samuels.

While I am very grateful to many people for the time spent with me sharing information, I am particularly indebted to several individuals for generous interview time and for comments on the substance of particular chapters. This includes Peter Goldmark, director of the New York Port Authority; Victor H. Palmieri, president of Victor Palmieri and Company; Professor Edward I. Altman, chairman of the Graduate School of Business Administration at New York University; Scott Kruse of Gibson, Dunn & Crutcher; and Con Howe, director of the Manhattan Office of the New York City Department of Planning. The manner in which their views are quoted or represented is solely the responsibility of the author.

Very early in the research for this book, I traveled to a small town in South Carolina to explore the effects of the bankruptcy of a privately owned textile mill. Three hundred and fifty employees had been laid off with two weeks notice and within days a pall had fallen on the small community which had come to rely on the economic contribution of its 100-year-old mill. The story of this bankruptcy does not appear in this book because it tells us little about what to do about a failing enterprise. The mill simply collapsed from its antiquated methods and from lost markets for its products. However, one of my many interviews in Newberry, South Carolina was with Talmadge Ellisor, a man who had devoted his life and career to the mill and who might normally have contributed another ten or fifteen productive years to his work as a plant supervisor. Talmadge's story expresses the saddest part of the business of bankruptcy. As an employee he was left literally "on the street" to fend like others with no support or pension from the firm to which he had devoted his life's emotions and energies.

His words and experiences provide an insight into the traumas often experienced by those involved in business bankruptcies. The words were shared in a small, neatly arranged bungalow behind his ranch house. Textiles had been his life since 1946. So dedicated was he to his work that he can count on one hand the number of days he was absent from work in thirty-five years. "Let's see when my daddy died; then my wife's daddy last year. He was eighty and still working at the mill. He fell one day and a few days later died all of a sudden just a day before my daughter's wedding a year ago.

"You know something, hours never bothered me. I worked as needed. If necessary I'd work a whole weekend to get a machine ready for work on Monday morning." And he added quickly, "Now I'm not complaining about it. That's just the way I was.

"The president was with six or seven of us one day not long ago and he said 'Who is Newberry Mills?' Nobody answered. He said 'It's you.' We knew month to month what was happening. I guess that I knew for almost three years that things were bad. I wouldn't let myself believe it. I was used to keeping my machines running in first-rate condition. But we weren't upgrading them and just let them run. Morale started getting low, especially when people realized that the general quality of the product was sliding down too.

"I really feel the owners turned their back on the company. Money was taken out of the company that should have stayed there to keep things up to date.

"At my age how I can I find a job. Nobody wants a 58-year-old man. Most of my friends from the mill are in the same boat. We've lost our company insurance. We have no pension benefits. They stopped paying the day I got my notice—that day! And they haven't paid me three weeks of accumulated vacation.

"I was that darn loyal to the company that I couldn't quit earlier. I couldn't turn my back on them and run. But they turned their back on me.

"I've left my entire future behind. To my three kids, my wife and I gave everything we had to pay for their education. That leaves us with no nestegg. Even now if I found work they'd start you out at minimum wages. And if they wanted me to move somewhere for a job I couldn't do it. At my age I could get a heart attack and then where would my wife be? The job she's got now is the only thing we've got to fall back on. She's a garment worker."

With a troubled look, Talmadge leaned forward rubbing his hands on his trousers and said: "Nothin's being bought. These old dungarees are getting thin. Know what I mean?

"The next cold spell will push," he says. "People like me will have to get food stamps—not because we want to. In this situation, you know, you think everything. During the day it's all right. It's at night when you lay down. You just roll and tumble. The longer it gets, the less I sleep at night. There don't seem to be answers in Newberry. And there are so many like me.

"I just want to be by myself. To think what to do. Nowadays I'm short tempered." With an awkward laugh he added, "the first thing that goes through your mind is to blow your brains out. I can't explain it."

This book is dedicated to Talmadge Ellisor.

Dan Dimancescu
1983

INTRODUCTION

T HE WRITING of this book was almost completed when, in April 1983, I arrived in Singapore on a business trip. On my first visit to this small island nation of two and a half million, I was unprepared to discover an environment as modern, well managed, and economically vibrant as the one forged in large part by Prime Minister Lee Kuan Yew during the last twenty years. His achievements have generated numerous references to Singapore as the new Switzerland of Asia. His economic successes are all the more impressive when one discovers that Singapore did it with only modest borrowings of foreign currency from the world market. Capital needed to build factories, roads, and sewers, and to create public services, an educational system, and an array of other needs was all generated from within the nation.

What was special about this revelation was that I had just come a few days earlier from Korea, which, although ten times larger in population, had borrowed almost $50 billion from foreign sources, or fifty times more than Singapore, to fuel its economic development. This kind of borrowing, much of it uncontrolled and in many cases far beyond the means of many borrowing nations to repay, had come to threaten the stability of the world economy. By the early 1980s many serious analysts of the international financial scene were acknowledging that a slow recovery from a world recession could have calamitous effects. Countries like Brazil, with almost $90 billion of accumulated debt and a limited ability to repay it even in the best of times, might default. Such actions—although staved off in 1983 by last-minute short-term efforts of world financial institutions—could lead to a chain reaction of financial failures worldwide or to politically disruptive events induced by harsh austerity measures needed to squeeze added foreign exchange out of a country's export economy.

On April 7, the day after my arrival in Singapore, the local newspaper headlined a story filed from São Paulo, Brazil. "Jobless go on the rampage in Brazil - Riots and looting as mobs clash with police." Army units were on alert in that giant city after mobs had torn down the iron fencing surrounding the state governor's palace. "Difficulties for the Brazilian poor," the article reported, "have been aggravated by a government austerity programme designed to prevent the government from defaulting on its US $83 billion foreign debt."

The message of three days of rioting was clear. The potential for political and economic upheaval, already explosive in Brazil, could easily spread to Mexico, Nigeria, Turkey, Poland, and a multitude of other nations tangled in a net of foreign debt and an increasing awareness that its repayment would be painful at best. The price of a decade's habit of excessive borrowing was beginning to be felt. Even if political unrest was not the catalyst, the unraveling might have happened as borrower nations bought fewer and fewer goods in the international marketplace, thereby inducing economic retrenchment in many seller developed nations.

The headline in the Singapore *Straits Times* caught my attention also because it explained the reason for writing this book. Like many Americans, I have watched in wonder at the compounding effect of inept leadership during the turbulent 1970s. The legacies of that decade leave us with an immense task of repairing, remolding, and rethinking the way in which our society and economy function in the world community. One aspect in particular called for far more explanation than seemed available. This was the phenomenal rise in the role debt would play as a means of growth and development for corporations and governments. Poland's indebtedness rose by 2,700 percent in ten years, Mexico's by 8,000 percent; corporations like W. T. Grant let debt rise by 3,000 percent in a few years; banks like Penn Square in Oklahoma allowed money to be loaned in ten-million-dollar multiples to individuals with no legally substantiated collateral to back it. These cases offer but a glimpse into a world of credit and debt gone haywire during the 1970s. Something had clearly gone out of control as one read about the bankruptcies of giant publicly held corporations all during the decade, the undeclared bankruptcy of New York City, and the defaults on interest and principal payments of many countries wallowing in unpayable debt.

Troubled by these events, I set out to explain why these conditions accelerated to such a point that the economic stability of the world was now put at risk. Part of what I discovered were the excesses of a new international cadre of world leaders—many of them financial experts or influenced by the advice of financiers—who had risen to power in corporations, banks, governments, and international institutions with a new and highly competitive attitude about the role of debt as a stimulant for growth. What they led us to, however, was a process of indebtedness that went uncontrolled and out of control. This book is in large part about the "decade of the financiers" and a rapid progression of events that started with the collapses of the Penn Central, one of America's largest blue-chip conglomerates in 1970; of New York City, the next-largest government to the federal government; and of Poland, Mexico, Brazil, and others by the end of the decade.

Bankruptcy became symptomatic of the problem of excessive debt and provided an insight into the mores and manipulations that now affect our economic well-being worldwide. The chapters that follow attempt to describe the escalation of a problem from its domestic setting to an international one and the role of formal bankruptcy as a mechanism for disentangling the burdens of debt. We discover that by the end of the decade the utility of bankruptcy as a juridical tool was lost as nations, themselves immune from any higher legal order, started to default on loans.

The saga of the 1970s was clearly to be remembered more for its blemishes than for its vision. During that decade America suffered through the withdrawal symptoms of its Vietnam debacle, the drug generation reached its peak, the oil crises disrupted the already fragile global financial structure, and most of the world—from the neighbor next door to the national finance ministries of all too many nations—indulged in a binge of indebtedness. This was the decade of go-go financial wizardry during which anyone with a feel for money—ministers, financiers, accountants, entrepreneurs, corporate boards, elected officials, bureaucracts, and everyday consumers—succumbed to the bright glow of easy-to-get credit.

The price of easy money from the friendly corner banker soon took its toll. "Businesses, large and small, are finding that the strategy of relying heavily on borrowed funds, widely pursued during the inflationary 1970's, has meant disaster and record rates of insolvency in a period of declining inflation," the *New York Times* observed.[1] This view, applicable not only to businesses but also to government institutions both in the United States and abroad, thrust the world financial system into a sudden awareness of its crystaline qualities. The borrowing that made payment of yesterday's loan cheaper with every increase in the inflationary index boomeranged with alarming speed as inflation slowed and debtors continued to hold loans at inordinantly high interest rates.

How did this insatiable appetite for debt rise to such unmanageable and uncontrolled proportions? The answer can be reduced to two simple hindsight observations: debt became a game unto itself, and debt took on a life of its own without any oversight or external means of restraint.

A business of debt evolved into a new, elaborate, and complex charade of pyramided card games in which the leading lending institutions played a pivotal role. A single dollar could leverage ten borrowed ones, and those in turn could lead to loans of one hundred more, and on and on. One of the most notorious American inventions during this period was the "moral obligation note"—the creation of John Mitchell, a man who acquired even greater notoriety as the attorney general of the United States under President Nixon. These notes offered an illusory *moral* guarantee of payment by public borrowers (cities and states) and opened the floodgates for new debt in states such as New York. By 1975 that state swam in such a thick pool of indebtedness that it took almost one year for a newly appointed budget director to trace how much was owed and who owed what to whom. Similarly, in a worldwide race to provide loans at competitive rates, banks allowed debt to be issued with little concern for the debtor's real means to repay either principal or interest. Short-term profits proved more alluring than repayment. Promises acquired more value than proof.

The second reason, which became evident as debtors as disparate as the Penn Central, W.T. Grant retailers, New York City, Poland, and Mexico proved insolvent, was an almost total absence of oversight restraints or guidelines on their borrowing habits. Not only had the debt become so complex that few could monitor it, but the process of enlarging debt obligation took on a life of its own. This laxity, pushed to extremes during the 1970s, shows no signs of being reversed as the federal government itself surges forward from its first $100 billion federal budgetary deficit in 1982 to predictions of double or triple that annual rate within a few years. The new deficits would remain faithful to an older dictum of spendthrift governments: If you don't have it, borrow and print it.

Lenders themselves helped blur the distinction between means to pay and ability to buy by flooding consumers with no-questions-asked credit cards; users indulged. Invented in 1950 by Diners Club, the modern credit card quickly matured into a basic means of trade, further distancing the act of indebtedness from the reality of the obligation incurred. American Express introduced its own version of easy plastic credit and subsequently unleashed a frenzy of other cards competing for the lucrative profits earned from up-front membership fees, interest on late payments, and fees from sellers of services to card holders.

"We want your business - badly" prevailed over conservative fiscal judgment not just with consumer credit in America but in commercial lending banks worldwide. In international markets for capital, a whole new currency metamorphosed outside of any single country's control—the Eurodollar. Its movements and manipulations exacerbated any rational attempts by central banks or international financial institutions to control a lending binge gone out of control. The intoxicating quick fix at the local bank spread to a multitude of government borrowers. As foreign indebtedness of all non-Communist developing nations rose from $90 billion in 1971 to an estimated $625 billion in 1982, threats of default unraveled another illusory pillar of financial stability: the country debtor as a "good risk."

The legacies of the 1970s, part of which are measured in the ballooning debt in all sectors of the world economy, finally hit home with increasing velocity as the economy slid into a recessionary cycle. A rising rate of bankruptcies quickly demolished a false front of stability to reveal a highly vulnerable inverted pyramid of debt. A by-product of these bankruptcies and insolvencies was the revelation of the inadequacies and failings of management in public and private institutions. Serious deficiencies in fiscal judgment surfaced, as did glaring abuses of elected officials' responsibility to protect the public interest. At issue also was the professionalism of lending institutions caught pandering to a borrowing clientele enamored with the quick fix of easy-to-get debt.

The 1980s would start with an urgent search for remedies. Poland was allowed to remain in undeclared default. The International Monetary Fund strong-armed new fund support from industrial nations to shore up Brazilian and Mexican debt. America twisted Japan's arm to lend a few more billion dollars to Korea. A consortium of fourteen American banks banded together to patch over a West Coast bank's failure. While no single global solution is yet forthcoming, discrete solutions to an internationally pervasive problem of unfettered debt are being tested in a patchwork of ad hoc measures.

What remains open for theorists and professional economists to resolve is a more basic reevaluation of the use and function of debt in modern economies. For sociologists and others, a field day is opening with novel attempts to redefine the role of money in modern cultures. Their task is to discover whether indeed there is a fundamental shift in attitudes accompanying the drift from a "cash only" economy to one based on credit. Their work acquires new urgency as the world verges on the mass distribution of "intelligent" credit cards. These little plastic cards will contain an individual's entire financial record and will permit a new generation of instant commercial transactions to occur. Purchases of goods and services, loans, deposits, and current statements will be recorded on the new wallet-size magic card. We are close to seeing such cards carrying the full financial record of a corporation within its micromemory. The shareholder, board director, and bank officer would thereby gain immediate access to data on a company's performance at any given moment. Would such information lead to greater rigor in corporate behavior or only further stimulate the growth of debilitating indebtedness?

This book provides a backdrop for the reader to begin to answer such questions. It offers an insight into the evolution of unmanaged debt from the corporate boardroom, to the nation's largest government institutions, to nations themselves. What ultimately links these three complex layers of borrowers is an inner core of large private lending institutions. The biggest of these are American banks, whose lending habits and behavior are central to an understanding of the new business of debt and bankruptcy. In some cases, their activities became more a matter of money-changing than of investment. They worried more about recycling dollars than about evaluating the credibility of investments. Their activities—and those of commercial and central banks in other major industrial powers—and their influence on our lives need to be understood because they play such a pivotal role in sustaining the non-Communist world's financial health.

To understand debt, therefore, is to understand a key determinant of our future well-being as contributors to and beneficiaries of a global economy. Indeed, the legacy of the 1970s challenged the very principle upon which debt is issued: the obligation to pay. Ironically, it was the lenders themselves who shared in accelerating the erosion of confidence and trust in the moral principle of repayment of financial obligations.

The stories that follow will help the reader understand some of the people, the behavior, and the effects of a decade during which *the act of indebtedness* lost its meaning. Many started asking whether debt was indeed meant to be repaid. Corporate bankruptcy offered a logical answer to the question for some; national default, the answer to others.

DEFERRED FUTURE

PART ONE

The Problem

Chapter 1

THE FINANCIERS' DECADE

THIS IS not a doomsday book. Perhaps it should have been. The world economic lifelines, stretched thin by a lingering recession, hold together by the tenuous ability of many nations to buy and sell one another's goods and services. One-quarter of our national economy is dependent on selling and buying goods to and from other countries. One out of twenty American manufacturing jobs depends on Third World purchases—countries who are unable to pay huge foreign debts or to sustain their buying habits from industrialized countries. How vulnerable we are is seen in the inability of these Third World nations to honor their payments on almost $600 billion in loans from the richer nations and their commercial banks, which issued more than 60 percent of it. The current price is paid in unemployed workers and stalled Third World economic development plans. The doomsday price would be a collapse of the world's leading banking institutions, the assets of which could be instantly eliminated by the default of a single borrower such as Brazil or Mexico.

What follows is a description of circumstances that brought us to a very fragile moment in our economic well-being. If this is not a doomsday scenario, it is because experiences have accumulated that still provide an opportunity to revive a weakened and overindebted world economy. Many answers come from more than a decade of unexpectedly large bankruptcies in the United States.

Events converged during the 1970s to cause a spree of insolvencies and bankruptcies by corporations and, by the decade's end, of nations. These events, from the flood of OPEC dollars starting in 1974, to an unprecedented escalation in interest rates, to an

3

unexpectedly long world recession, revived an age-old lament: "If I could just borrow a little more all my problems would be solved." Nowadays the lament comes in billion-dollar doses. And surprisingly, it works. It seems that the more you ask for, the more you are likely to get.

If there was a new concern about the ageless business of moneylending, it was that more and more money was lent on thinner and thinner means of repayment and with less and less external oversight over borrowing habits. To the outside world looking in on the banking profession something definitely seemed to have gone wrong. Consider the case in 1982—a time when country defaults started swirling through newspaper headlines—of the Bankers Trust of South Carolina bank, a small regional lending institution. That year it issued a six-month loan of $5 million to Mexico only to be told when it was due that no repayment would be made. The lender's original decision to issue the loan, based on three-year-old data issued to him by the International Monetary Fund (IMF), was heavily swayed by major lending banks in New York. They were "most avid recommenders," said the lending officer, Richard Fearrington, to a reporter from the *Wall Street Journal*. From Mexican officials he received word that the nation's foreign currency reserves rose by $7.3 billion up to $10.3 billion by August 1981. Yet its foreign debt had risen by $11.4 billion in the same year—and would rise by $8 billion more within another three months alone! The latter was not reported. Bankers Trust was now the proud owner of a $5 million loan that it had no choice but to keep renewing, or rolling over, as the process is commonly termed.

In Mexico, a powerful private banker volunteered to a *World Paper* reporter: "We were as conned as anyone else, and we also did a major part of the conning. Sure, we've been guilty of avarice, of losing sight of the financial forest for the fruit-bearing trees."

In 1983, the United States had to increase its contributions to the IMF by more than $8 billion just to shore up temporarily the debts of many Third World countries. The same year, Korea asked for $4 billion more and got it; Mexico got $5 billion from a consortium of 540 banks and quickly announced that it needed another $7 billion. Brazil, Argentina, Poland, Romania, and a variety of others are asking for billions more—and getting it. Equivalent corporate cases abound. Take the example of Baldwin-United Corp., a Cincinnati conglomerate that includes the famed Baldwin piano makers, which bought an insurance company in 1982 for $1.2 billion. Half of these funds were borrowed. Within less than a year of this acquisition, the company was unable to meet a scheduled repayment of $440 million owed by a subsidiary, Balunit. The parent's short-term debt totaled more than twice that amount. The effects on the rise and fall of this accountant's dream firm was a stock price chart that looked like a seismic shock. In fact, Baldwin-United paid an immense premium to buy nothing other than time in a transaction of worthless short-term value. On Wall Street a Baldwin watcher reportedly said: "If Baldwin can work out a debt-repayment plan and hold on to its new acquisition until times get better, ten years from now it will look like a stroke of genius." A decade is a very long time for a bank to wait patiently to get its money back.

It is sobering to note that the bankers whose money was at risk—most of it belonging to their shareholders and depositors—did not bother to study the credibility of the Baldwin proposition. What they would have found is a corporate history of illusory "paper profits" based on anticipated effects of tax credits due to the company. A little more prying would have revealed a company functioning at an operating loss, meaning that it was taking in less than it was paying out.

Such mistakes, repeated hundreds of times during the 1970s and into the early 1980s, explain in part the crisis of debt facing the world today. Many are the result of spurious decisions by modern financiers to lend large cumulative amounts of capital with minimal attention to the means of repayment by an avid array of sophisticated borrowers. Many of them are due, too, to the deliberate speculations of bonds dealers who, for a number of years, promoted high yields to potential buyers while knowing full well the damaging effects of inflation on the value of bonds. It is explained, too, in a widespread corporate belief that borrowed money does not detrimentally dilute equity or ownership control. Thus, as money became more easily available early in the 1970s, many corporations saw an ideal opportunity for expansion and rapid growth without the onerous price of relinquishing ownership. A faculty member of the Harvard Business School, William Sahlman, calls this "the biggest red herring in corporate biases I've ever seen. It doesn't take much to see that the lender can very quickly become far more intrusive in corporate affairs than the shareholder."

A national and international thirst for debt is partly understood also by a change in the character of the successful manager in the modern corporate world. It was not that long ago that production line expertise could easily propel an ambitious manager to the top of his firm. During the 1950s and 1960s that changed. The path upward shifted to the advantage of marketeers who boosted consumerism to new heights—from TV sets to soap suds. By the end of the 1960s that too changed. It was now the turn of the corporate finance officer. Numbers people, as they were soon labeled, acquired new status. This was due in part to the masterful performance of financial and accounting experts such as Harold S. Geneen, who led the International Telegraph and Telephone Corporation into becoming a powerful global multinational. Geneen became the accountant's role model at the corporate helm and the message filtered into business schools, where finance and accounting quickly became essential M.B.A. requisites to corporate success.

By the early 1980s, power and influence had shifted from those most intimately linked to the day-to-day production line workings of companies and institutions to those better skilled in quantitative analytical arts—especially those having to do with the highly specialized art of financial management. Often, financial wizardry generated quicker profits than the much harder task of developing a better product on the shop floor. The lesson was not lost in government circles, where power fell more and more into the hands of those able to perform the "magic" of financing ever-rising expenditures. For local governments this meant imaginative borrowing formulas to hire more employees and pay for more costly services. For national governments this meant borrowed

money to buy exotic and costly weapons, new production technologies for local industries, expensive consultants, and vital
energy resources to fuel machines, trucks, and power plants.
As finance—or paper entrepreneurship, as Harvard economist
Robert Reich calls it—replaced production as a key to
profitability, a discovery was made. Money could be borrowed—
or leveraged as some prefer to say—to play all sorts of new games.
One of the favorites was the acquisition game illustrated by the
Balwin-United fiasco. Yesterday's firm with relatively small sales
revenues and modest profitability could buy a new cash-rich
company and reemerge in next year's annual report double its size
and ever more profitable—on paper. Wall Street would notice the
upward incline of the total pooled sales and new upward
profitability curve and, like oil on water, word would spread of the
successful new investor opportunity. Stocks would be traded, the
per share price would rise, and glowing articles would follow in
business periodicals. In fact, nothing would have changed except
on paper. Rarely would the productivity of a particular division or
the quality of a given product have changed.

Adding fuel to the process was the unexpected rise in influence
of OPEC. Banding together, the member countries managed in
the early 1970s to force buyer countries to pay ever higher prices
for crude oil. Prices shot upward and caused an upheaval in the
world economy—brought home to Americans in nightly television
shots of long lines of cars waiting impatiently for a turn at the gas
pump. One result was a surge in cash profits to OPEC's national
coffers. All of this money was deposited by its new owners into
banks throughout the world. Idle money has little value to a
banker, and they quickly went to work "recycling" this immense
and growing pool of oil profits. The result was a buyers' market in
which money was available for the asking and in which bankers
fought head-on among themselves to offer it at competitive rates.
In this competitive setting little concern for the credit worthiness
of the borrower absorbed the attention of the anxious banker.

As interest rates escalated, borrowing "short" for periods less
than a year became a financial modus operandi. Not wanting to get
stuck holding expensive debt too long, borrowers asked for 30-,

60-, or 90-day notes rather than for one or more years' duration; they learned to play with new ways of manipulating corporate cash to earn cash from rising interest rates. Cash management became a new professional skill. Within a few years, considerable corporate creativity focused solely on financial transactions and ignored more basic corporate needs—e.g., for new equipment, repairs, and product research and development, all of which were now costing more as inflation raised replacement prices year by year. The cumulative effect was dismaying.

By 1983, the problem of indebtedness reached international crisis proportions. Third World countries held in excess of 600 percent more debt than they did a decade earlier. And as more of it came due, less repayment was honored. In 1983, banking spokesmen such as Robert McNamara, ex-head of the World Bank, suggested that we were witnessing nothing other than a passing crisis. Many others saw the world living on dangerously fragile borrowed time. An ongoing recession and a single unexpected default at the wrong place and wrong time could collapse the world economy and lead it headlong into a depression. In May of the same year, U.S. Treasury Secretary Donald T. Regan warned a Paris audience of financiers of "unpleasant difficulties" if strong measures were not taken to bail out many Third World debtors.

"International lending has become a mine field of rolled over debt," wrote the *Wall Street Journal*[1] as foreign news repeatedly sent shudders throughout U.S. financial institutions. Fueling this rising tide of alarm was a three-year period during which lending rates to developing countries grew at 21 percent a year. "These rates of growth for loans," the Morgan Guaranty Bank announced, "far outstripped those of bank capital." In addition, heavy borrowing by Mexico, Brazil, Argentina, and South Korea resulted in increasing concentration of bank credit among a few nations.[2] Their failure to pay their obligations in any one year would topple America's nine largest banks. Citicorp of New York is deeply enmeshed in Brazil; the First National Bank of Boston is the biggest American lender in Argentina.

For the less fortunate "one-crop" or "one-commodity" less developed nations, the problem of surging debt burdens is bleak. Few have any prospects of whittling away at large debt aggravated by interest rates that are no longer affordable. "What we have is an international debt blockage," says Henry Kaufman, chief economist at Salomon Brothers. "Unless it is resolved soon, it will hamper economic recovery. It is not a temporary problem, but an on-going one that requires structural change to fix it."[3]

Political tensions and open warfare in some regions did little to alleviate the trepidation rippling through world financial centers. The Iran crisis gave way to the Polish economic collapse, and then to the potential default by Argentina on its own $34 billion in foreign debt as it diverted its cash resources to pay for the Falklands war. But of the three, it is the Polish crisis that proffered the most controversial prospects for U.S. and Western banks. With a debt totaling more than $27 billion, Poland was unable in 1980 to meet its interest payments or to honor any payment on the principal amounts due. American banks, members of a loosely affiliated international financial consortium of 500 affected lending institutions, stood to lose almost a sixth of that amount. Three years later, despite the clear evidence of Poland's inability to honor its debt, the principal and interest still remained classified in bank books as "good loans."

From coast to coast within the United States bankers reluctantly admitted to the possibility of a financial collapse. In the United States alone, bank loans outstanding for oil exploration totaled $33 billion—an amount three times higher than only five years before.[4] The Federal Reserve Board estimates that of a total business debt of $135 billion in the largest commercial banks, 17.6 percent in 1982 was devoted to oil extraction and refining. The effect of prices declining by 7 percent in the first two years of the 1980s and further downward in 1983 is significant; the first unavoidable signal of danger became evident in the failed Penn Square Bank in Oklahoma City—even though fraudulent actions may share a large part of the blame. From Knoxville to Tulsa and Seattle, the thinness of the line separating the solvents from the insolvents became clear. During the first half of 1983, seven Tennessee banks were declared insolvent by the state's banking commissioner. In Oklahoma, forty-seven banks were listed as risky by state monitoring agencies. Others, such as Seafirst Corporation in Seattle, incurred such high losses that $1.5 billion in emergency support was provided earlier in the year by a group of fourteen banks—themselves hoping to avoid a cascading series of bank failures.

What might go wrong? More than a decade of indebtedness accumulated during the roller-coaster 1970s finally caught up. The whiplash of rags to riches is illustrated by the performance of one oil-drilling equipment company, Nucorp Energy, Inc. In the year 1980 to 1981, its revenues multiplied 425 percent, from $91 million to $461 million; its stock, worth $1 per share in 1978, jumped to $20. Yet, less than a year after these heady results, the company filed for bankruptcy after defaulting on $300 million in debts. Like many others, the company got caught gambling the repayment of its debts on future high oil prices—$35 per barrel for domestic oil in 1981, up from $12.64 a year earlier. When prices suddenly slid downward it found itself with unsalable inventories and many competitors with the same problem.

Company bankruptcy filings rose steeply in 1980, 1981, and again in 1982 as the recessionary effects intensified; the rate of 47,000 in 1981 was four times higher than the average annual rate for the prior twenty-five years. By late 1982, the rate was 47 percent higher than a year earlier, reaching levels not equaled since 1933. Corporate failures occurred at a rate of more than thirty every business hour of the year. Even billion-dollar liability failures became common enough no longer to raise eyebrows on Wall Street. As the nation teetered between hopes of economic recovery and painful depression, bankruptcy offered clear symptoms of how fragile the financial structure had really become.

Even in the best of years, the bankruptcy statistics ring alarm bells. Yet, a broad scan of the last one hundred years shows failure statistics falling into two significantly different phases. From 1870 until 1930, with the brief exception of a two-year period after World War I, the rate of business bankruptcies remained three to four times higher than between 1930 and 1980—an average rate of one-hundred failures per ten thousand firms compared with an average rate closer to twenty-five or thirty during the last fifty years. In 1878 and again in 1932, times of extreme economic crisis, the rate jumped as high as 158 and 154 failures per ten thousand companies. During the peak of the depression, the losses incurred from bankruptcies equaled almost 2 percent of the GNP—a percentage forced upward by a GNP that dropped from $90.7 billion in 1930 to a gaunt $58.3 billion two years later.

Since World War II, however, the financial losses incurred from business failures have remained consistently low in relation to the GNP—fluctuating between one-fourth and one-fifth of one percent. Even with dramatic increases in the rate of failure registered in the early 1980s, the relationship to GNP remained relatively low and constant. Thus, in 1980, despite liability claims of failed companies in excess of $4.5 billion, and $6 billion in 1981, the net effect in an economy with a $2,500 billion to $3,000 billion GNP remained relatively constant and minor.

Even if the signposts of business failure—which showed ominous increases in 1981, 1982, and 1983—were still safely within ranges that the economy could cushion, more troublesome to the world of investors and bankers was the unexpected vulnerability of large publicly held companies. The Penn Central collapse in June 1970, while probably a natural outcome of the railroad operation's astounding inefficiency, was a forerunner of much more to come. Other giant firms have since taken the plunge into the litigious world of bankruptcy courts during the ensuing decade. Among them are such notable companies as the equipment-leasing firm, Itel, with 19,200 shareholders and $1.7 billion in liabilities; Wickes Cos., with 26,079 shareholders and $2 billion in liabilities; and Braniff International, with a $1 billion plus debt and 33,000 shareholders. During the first thirty months of the 1980s, seventy-six publicly held firms—with names as familiar as Lionel, Advent, Bobbie Brooks, and Sambo's—filed for legal bankruptcy protection. This put them into the hands of federal bankruptcy courts and immediately halted any creditors' claims until a settlement was agreed to by all parties. Just these few giant companies' cumulative liabilities exceeded $10 billion, or almost 80 percent of the total declared liabilities for all failed businesses during that two-and-half-year period. This economic burden, concentrated to such a high degree in a few companies, has new and far-reaching implications. The most evident is that the effects of a single bankruptcy, no longer diluted among many smaller business firms, could more easily topple a national financial house of cards.

Corporate insolvencies and bankruptcies are hardly a uniquely American habit. Even in nonrecessionary times, Japanese failures of companies have been four times higher than in the United States, reflecting, in part, a far more vulnerable pool of very small businesses in the economic mainstream. In Europe, bankruptcy rates surged upward in the 1980s. From 1980 through 1981 in West Germany alone—Europe's miracle economy—they rose an unprecedented 27.4 percent; and another 40 percent the subsequent year.[5] While such statistics produced a steady stream of press headlines, many people were unprepared during the summer of 1982 for the receivership bankruptcy of one of West Germany's largest conglomerates: AEG-Telefunken. With a worldwide work-force of 123,000 and an additional 150,000 dependent on the firm as suppliers in Germany alone, the giant electrical firm's woes, including $2.2 billion in outstanding debt, startled European financial capitals. The timing could not have been worse as German and other European banks simmered in the realization that Poland could do little to honor more than $27 billion in foreign debts, much of it from West German banks.

The U.S. federal government itself has accumulated a trillion dollars of debts to its domestic lenders in a 250 percent climb of new debt since 1970. In 1982, the annual federal deficit rate set new records as it surpassed the unprecedented $100 billion mark—an escalation that systematically ignored legislated ceilings on the permissible level of accumulated national debt. Despite such legislated attempts at fiscal restraint or even a fervent ideological Republican commitment to a balanced budget fiscal policy, the Reagan administration's budgetary practices will propel the deficit to new heights. During his administration alone, the deficits will exceed the cumulative amount of *all* other U.S. presidents. The effect will be to force interest rates back up at exactly the time when a recovery depends on their going down. An added irony is that the "Buy now. Pay later." philosophy that conservatives decry in the predicted bankruptcy of the nation's New Deal social security system is the very one they urge in building a new generation of ever more expensive weaponry.

Even within the United States Treasury Department there exists laxity of public oversight. Its Federal Financing Bank is allowed to guarantee and issue debt as a result of what are termed "off-budget" items first authorized in 1973 under President Nixon's administration. One finds here almost $130 billion of outstanding loans. Ten percent of these are issued to finance arms purchases by almost fifty countries—the largest borrowers including Israel and Egypt, the smallest including Zaire. Such loans are issued at the request of any federal agency, in this case the Department of Defense, with presidential approval. The preponderant amount goes directly to other agencies for such activities as the Tennessee Valley Authority or the Import-Export Bank, or to projects designated by an agency, such as railroads, hospitals, and housing. Guarantees of politically sensitive foreign nation debts, such as Zaire or Pakistan, are insulated from any public oversight constraints. The size of its commitments could hardly be gleaned from a one-line mention of its name on page 644 of the official 900-page government manual, which devotes twenty-five pages elsewhere to its parent, the Treasury Department. As a knowledgeable observer, not wishing to be identified, puts it, "you get into some pretty hairy financing when one looks into that bank."

The concept of paying tomorrow what is consumed today is an infectious one endemic to the culture. Consumers owe far in excess of $1 trillion to their creditors for everything from home mortgages to department store purchases. When seen in a thirty-year perspective, this consumer debt shows no signs of abatement. While personal incomes have risen 250 percent in real dollars during that post-World War II period, the rate of personal indebtedness rose twice as fast—one explanation for the spiraling rate of recorded personal bankruptcies during the past few recessionary years.

Liberalization of personal bankruptcy laws in 1978, making it easier for an individual to file and to retain assets, and the impacts of a deepened recession are seen by some as catalysts for the doubling of personal bankruptcies during the past three to four years. One effect of a huge and tenuous rise in consumer indebtedness is intensified pressure on Congress to tighten the laws against individuals who are seen as having easy access to legally forgiven debt.

The cumulative effect of the debt burdens of the United States and global economy is an intensified and unspoken fear that the worst could indeed happen. As Felix Rohatyn admonished: "Our democratic system will be challenged unless economic policy is reviewed and action taken."[6] His words would be echoed by the governor of São Paulo, Franco Montoro, who, in reference to three days of rioting in the spring of 1983 over rigid Brazilian austerity measures, told the press "those kinds of provocations represent the beginning of movements that destroy democracies in various parts of the world."[7]

The traditional remedy, a resort to formal bankruptcy, needs to be understood if one is to grapple with the dilemma of debt. Not only did custom evolve into a set of laws that mediated the domestic conflict that pits creditor against debtor, but it nurtured a set of very practical conceptual tools to which we now turn.

Chapter 2

A LONG JOURNEY

insolvent: *In general usage, an inability to pay one's debts as they fall due. According to U.S. Federal law, a person is insolvent if the sum of his or her property, at fair valuation, is not sufficient to pay his or her debts.*

—Dictionary of Business Economics

bankrupt: *A person, corporation, or other legal entity which, being unable to meet its financial obligations has been declared by a decree of the court to be insolvent, and whose property becomes liable to administration under the Bankruptcy Reform Act of 1978.*

—Dictionary of Banking & Finance

INSOLVENCY IS a problem, bankruptcy a solution. Yet, according to these definitions neither Poland nor any other country could be considered bankrupt since there is no court that could legally declare it so, nor could it be termed insolvent because its assets, meaning its land and physical capital, are technically worth far in excess of its debts. Despite such definitional problems, the terms are commonly used to describe the widespread phenomenon of national indebtedness. The terminology is far more precise, however, in defining the dilemma of numerous American cases of corporations and individuals going broke.

The advantage of treating bankruptcy as a barometer of the debt crisis nationally and worldwide is that it may offer useful clues on how to solve and perhaps even help inhibit uncontrolled borrowing in the future. Two conceptual innovations—translated into America's first permanent bankruptcy laws ninety years ago—help frame the way in which debtor problems are commonly resolved. One is the "second-chance" notion. This idea, now firmly embedded in our beliefs and laws, holds that a person, corporation, or public entity buried in debt should have an opportunity for a fresh, unfettered start. It is better, common sense has taught us over the centuries, to have a productive member of a community than one punished and banished from further social or economic intercourse.

The second conceptual innovation is that a debtor be allowed, where possible, to settle debts for a small portion of their original value. This belief is now normal practice with individuals and corporations, and it goes unchallenged as part of the juridical process of settlement. It is far from agreed, however, that the same principle should apply to indebted nations defaulting on their obligations. The latter is a subject that invites considerable debate in international financial circles. Subsequent chapters will explore it in detail. Commercial banks, in search of a way to unburden themselves of the immense foreign loans they have issued, would welcome settlements, but rarely do they suggest that it be done at their expense.

Before attempting to answer the question of how to settle national indebtedness, a brief explanation of the long journey that brought bankruptcy laws into being may give more breadth to one's understanding of the contemporary debt crisis. At present in the United States much of it is acted out before 227 federal bankruptcy judges. Their workload, if one includes individual filings, totaled 700,000 pending cases at the end of 1982, with 10,000 cases being added weekly. For Prudence Beatty Abram, a newly appointed bankruptcy judge, the novelty of the challenge facing her was largely in the backlog of large corporate cases. "This is an exciting time to be involved in bankruptcy cases," she suggested. "In the last few years much more use has been made of the bankruptcy code by large nationally known corporations. These obviously are very interesting cases."[1]

But what by the 1980s had become a complex legal process in which debtor and creditor faced one another on relatively equal footing—some now argue that the debtor holds too great an advantage—has not always been so. The history of bankruptcy, and that aspect that focuses on the plight of the corporation, is a lengthy and tortuous story. It leads from a point in history when debt was considered immoral and a debtor in trouble had no rights or legal recourse, to a point in the present where it is the creditor who is arguing his own loss of rights or recourse against the debtor. This era spans almost two thousand years of slow evolution and frequent regressions to punitive and harsh retribution against the debtor.

If at present the penalty of debt is measured mainly in sleepless nights, valiums, and ulcers, there was a time in the United States when a business failure brought on harsh legal penalties and engraved deep, permanent personal scars—many of them suffered in cheerless prison cells. It was not that long ago that the creditor had full recourse to one-sided laws allowing ruthlessly successful collection efforts. There was the case two hundred years ago, for example, of Robert Morris, one of the Revolutionary War's major financiers. He was left to sit sullenly for three years in the Prune Street debtors' prison in Philadelphia. His unpaid debts amounted to the then whopping sum of $12 million. His woes, induced by a severe financial collapse of unrestrained real estate speculations in 1797, were shared by many others. The crisis swallowed up enterprises like the Yazoo Company, the purchaser of 30 million acres covering most of present-day Mississippi and Alabama; another disaster, the North American Land Company, controlling 6 million acres in New York, Pennsylvania, and in the South, crumbled, sealing the fate of many investors including Robert Morris. Most bankrupts shared the ignominy of debtors' prisons.

Such unfortunates, some of whom were pardoned of their debts during a brief reprieve in 1800, would have to wait until 1821 for the first state laws abolishing emprisonment for unpaid debt to be passed first in Kentucky, followed a decade later by New York and a flurry of other states. By 1857, when Massachusetts eliminated prison terms, unless fraud could be demonstrated, the worst punitive manifestations of a creditor's wrath came to a close in America.

But if America was in the first throes of evolving its laws to be more compassionate and understanding of the debtor-creditor relationship, tales and fears of more gruesome and severe punish-

17

ment in other parts of the world sustained the aura of fear and shame associated with financial collapse. Even by century's end, when a permanent American bankruptcy law would finally be passed, newspapers indulged in sharing the more lurid examples of failure. In Siam, one newspaper reported at that time, a debtor who did not make sure to depart his nation ahead of his creditors would be jailed with his entire family until the monies owed were paid. In China "all delinquents pass into a dishonored class and are soon put to punishment by bamboo blows." A debt of $5,000 or more in the 1890s could be settled by decapitation.[2] In Russia the punishment for fraudulent bankruptcies was the ever-useful one-way banishment to Siberia. In Switzerland one lost all civil rights.

A more imaginative penalty was invented during the sixteenth century by the French, who required that a debtor wear a green bonnet. In Scotland a similar law imposed a dress of brown or yellow coats. Yet, though mellower, such penalties did more than bruise personal reputations and egos; they reinforced deep-rooted moral beliefs about the evils of indebtedness. These were clearly evident in Protestant and Puritan England, where in 1542 the first laws addressing bankruptcy were passed by Parliament in an "acte againste suche persones as doo make Bankrupte." It spared no words or imagery in describing the evils of debt.

> Whereas divers and sundry persons, craftily obtain into their own hands great substance of other men's goods, do suddenly flee to parts unknown, or keep their houses, not mindful to pay or restore to any of their creditors, their debts and duties, but at their own wills and pleasures consume the substance obtained by credit of other men, for their own pleasure and delicate living, against all reason, equity and good conscience.[3]

It would take a few more centuries for bankruptcy to turn the tide on such deep-rooted emotions—almost universally shared irrespective of geography or culture. The slow tide of change would span the very first attempts by Roman jurists to mediate the debtor-creditor dilemma, to the most recent comprehensive legislative bankruptcy amendments enacted by the U.S. Congress in 1978.

An American Solution

It was not always self-evident that a "second-life" could be found in the assets of a bankrupt. Rather, during the long struggle that led to a permanent bankruptcy law in the United States, the press, politicians, and outspoken moralists had an open field for their notions about the evils of indebtedness. As late as 1897, during the final stages of debating the famed Torrey Bill, which is the foundation of today's bankruptcy laws, a noted journal *The Nation* illustrated the feelings frequently vented against the worst offenders.

> That dishonest insolvents constitute a large and conspicuous class in the community cannot be disputed. Almost every one has a few among his acquaintances, whom he meets driving in the Park, or observes drinking champagne at Delmonico's. . . . Indeed the comic books make insolvency one of the high roads to fortune, which would be impossible in a community in which dishonest insolvency was looked upon with horror.[4]

But if disdain for a minority of unscrupulous financial manipulators did indeed have a place, it would play a large role in delaying the drafting of legislation focused on the financial failure and accompanying calamities of merchants, corporations, and individuals. More persuasive catalysts were the jagged cycles of rags to riches linked to recessionary economic cycles. Frequent depressions would invite fervent calls for laws to protect debtors. On three occasions Congress passed legislation in response to such economic crises. In 1800 a law was passed, the first of its kind for the new republic. It lasted three years. A subsequent boom in the nation's export economy defused the need for a national law and successfully fueled the opposition to a law. But within a few years, restrictive French and British trade policies would intentionally discriminate against the use of American cargo ships; to this was coupled the ruinous impact of the Embargo and Non-Intercourse Acts of Presidents Jefferson and Madison. "Debts piled up," writes historian Charles Warren, "and the jails were filled to overflowing with imprisoned debtors."[5] Times were so bad that, between 1815 and 1819 alone, there was a shrinkage of currency in circulation of 50 percent. A Baltimore paper would decry the apathy prevailing in Congress by asking: "How long will they shut their ears against the cries of distress? How long will they neglect supplications of thousands?"[6]

During this period of economic distress repeated efforts were made to legislate a bankruptcy law. During the 16th Congress, by an ever so slight tilt in voting, a historic precedent was almost established. For the first time, an amendment had been proposed that would speak to the needs of debtors rather than favoring creditors' efforts to gain hold of merchant and trader property. The proposed law suggested that those imprisoned for unpaid debts have the right to file a voluntary petition to be declared bankrupt—and thereby be released of their financial burdens. A fervent supporting speech by Henry Clay of Kentucky helped pass the historic amendment. But the victory proved Pyrrhic. The full bankruptcy bill—with sixty-four detailed sections—was defeated by northerners who viewed the measure as unconstitutional and southerners who opposed any sort of law on the subject.

The debate blew hot and tempestuous for almost thirty subsequent years. Finally, in the wake of another calcifying financial collapse labeled the "two-dollars-for-one" economy by one legistator, another law was passed in 1841, this time induced into being by the surging numbers of debtors. Political observers of the time saw the power of the Whig party, victorious in the 1840 presidential election of John Tyler, founded in the escalated ranks of an estimated 400,000 bankrupts nationwide. Ralph Waldo Emerson would write in his diary: "None calleth us to labor. . . . The present generation is bankrupt of principles and hope, as of property."[7]

The beginnings of a familiar ditty "ten cents on the dollar" would soon become part of the bankruptcy lore. Hardly a year old, the freshly circulated bankruptcy law allowed more than 33,500 people to find aid in their distress. Their collective debts of $450 million were settled with creditors for one-tenth that amount. After administrative costs charged by the federal courts, little would be left to trickle down to distraught or disillusioned creditors.

But the fickleness of two years was quickly evident. Inadequacies in technicalities of the law, renewed prosperity in the land, and a regrouped opposition won the day. The new law was once again repealed. The absence of a governing federal law on the subject of bankruptcy was ameliorated by the passage by many states of laws offering even stronger protection for the individual debtor. These included measures, outlined earlier, to abolish prison terms and to inhibit drastic action by creditors by delaying their attempts to take control over the assets of debtors. One constraint that states were powerless to overcome, however, was the inability of a state court to discharge a debtor's liability to a creditor in another state. The need for a uniform set of federal standards abiding on states remained.

Once again, the economy plummeted in 1857. Difficult times would sustain the call for new laws until the Civil War. Midwestern states tallied the greatest losses from bankruptcies—three times that of the commercial northeastern states. But the latter would soon suffer worsening fortunes as the secession of the South worked its own magic by eliminating the farming South's large debts to the northern merchants and their banks. Of an estimated $300 million owed by plantation owners and their associated traders, one-half was due to New York City banks, one-tenth to Philadelphia banks, and lesser amounts to Baltimore and Boston institutions. In New York City in 1861 almost 1,000 mercantile houses became insolvent; out of 256 dry-goods establishments only 6 percent were solvent at year's end. Diverted by the war, Congress failed to act in any way to legislate a protective measure. These collapses would explain in part the emotional fervor of the carpetbaggers' return to the South at the war's end.

Occasional debates on the subject of a new law introduced the novel idea of bringing corporations under the protection of bankruptcy laws. Such a step would prove far reaching in broadening the protection of the courts not only from merchants and traders to ordinary individuals, but also to what one tentative bill entitled "moneyed, business, or commercial corporations."[8]

The war years passed. New economic crises prevailed, and a

third bankruptcy act was legislated into law in 1867. It would endure a decade. Finally, however, its demise was sealed by a vote of 250 to 40 in the House of Representatives. In the Senate, William P. Whyte of Maryland would rationalize the defeat by arguing that the act "had accomplished its mission." A colleague from Kentucky would embellish its rejection by calling the act an "assault upon public morals, in its violations of good faith, in its craft, in its falsehoods and frauds." Extensive abuses by federal courts—in particular in southern states vulnerable to the vices of carpetbagging and score settling between northern "Yankee" traders and "rebel" debtors—sustained a widely held image of abuse and dishonesty that would cloud renewed initiatives to pass a more permanent law.[9]

Not until 1890 did a serious discussion resume on the merits of a national bankruptcy law. The absence of a law governing so commonplace a phenomenon as business failure and an inability to pay debts was widely viewed as an absurdity in the new republic. Several decades earlier, one of those most eloquent in his call for a permanent measure was Senator Daniel Webster, who argued before his colleagues:

> The result is bad every way. It is bad for the public and the country, which loses the efforts and industry of so many useful and capable citizens. It is bad for creditors, because there is no security against preferences, no principal of equality, and no encouragement for honest, fair and reasonable assignments of effects.[10]

The whiplashing zig-zag of efforts to bring a law into being in the United States exposed deeply felt instincts about the rights and wrongs of indebtedness and the economic conditions that invite it. The farmer's economic well-being was central to these arguments. Time and again it was argued that the farmer lived a production cycle that required indebtedness early in the planting season to pay for grain and repayment only after crops were sold. Subject to the vicissitudes of nature, most farmers could hardly predict the bounty of their labors. Floods, droughts, disease, or economic downturns could strike deathly blows to the most industrious and assiduous farmer. Thus, it was argued, a law that favored harsh treatment of the farmer by treating his land as a disposable asset available on demand to his creditors would shatter the very foundation of the nation's stability.

By 1898, legislators would compromise by agreeing to exclude farmers and laborers from involuntary actions against them by creditors. Along the way, though, some of the most virulent political speeches were those of politicians speaking out for farmers and the nonmonied classes. An example was a congressman from Alabama, William H. Denson, who spoke out in 1893 against a bankruptcy bill that favored creditors as "an infernal engine of ruin, slavery, and destruction to the masses, another cruel and destructive instrumentality employed by the demon Money to crush out the farmers, the laborers and the masses of the country and make them subservient to the. ... Money Power of this land."[11]

A hundred years earlier Thomas Jefferson had argued a similar position by asking: Is commerce "so much the basis of the existence of the United States as to call for a bankrupt law? On the contrary," he said, "are we not almost agricultural? Should not all laws be made with a view essentially to the poor husbandman?"[12] The debate would pit merchants against farmers, manufacturers against bankers, and industrial cities against farming regions.

However slowly, the makings of a bankruptcy law wove through the emotional web of regional politics and special interest lobbying. A compelling motive to devise a coherent set of rules traced back to a mandate drafted into the text of the Constitution. Under the clauses that outline the powers of Congress to regulate commerce is the vesting in Congress of power to pass "uniform laws on the subject of Bankruptcies."[13] At the time it was drafted, in 1787, the sole dissenting vote was from Roger Sherman of Connecticut. He objected to a possible grant of powers that might lead to punishment of bankruptcies by death, as some earlier British laws had allowed. But for constitutional theorists it was long unresolved whether this clause was intended to apply to merchants and traders, as in the English laws, or whether it might absorb all classes of people, as did some American states in their own laws.

The Making of a Law

A new set of laws was drafted in 1890 by a young attorney from St. Louis named Jay L. Torrey. His efforts would set off a seven-year legislative struggle. Against his most vocal opponents, mostly southerners and westerners who spoke for their economically fragile farm constituencies, Torrey repeated a flowery and empassioned plea.

> When a vessel is laboring at sea nothing will more surely sink her than to leave untouched the broken masts and loose spars which every wave is using as a battering ram to pound her to pieces and carry her to the bottom. She can be saved only by cutting away the wreckage. That relief is what the absence of a bankruptcy law denies to the businessman overtaken by a storm of disaster.[14]

The Torrey Bankruptcy Bill eventually was submitted to Congress in 1896. It was approved by the 55th Congress two years later. In the Senate the vote was a decisive 49 to 8; in the House, 159 to 125. The chairman of the House Judiciary Committee, Ezra B. Taylor, lauded the bill as "remarkable for the terseness of its style, the fairness to both debtor and creditor of its provisions, and the expedition and economy it will necessitate in the settlement of estates."[15] On July 1, 1898, President McKinley signed it into law.

Perhaps because of its unusual clarity and its evenhandedness, the act would endure. Early efforts to defeat it soon after the turn of the century never again regained the momentum of earlier opposition. It has been amended almost one hundred times, major revisions being made in 1938 and in 1978. Its evolution reflects changes affecting the country itself and the rising maturity of America's new industrial and commercial economy. Its most significant contribution may have been the final realization that the national interest was best served by ensuring the survival of an individual's or a corporation's material well-being. It established an irrefutable common link between the rehabilitation of a debtor and the interests of the creditor. Such a conception, farseeing as it was, would permanently bury the long-standing view that a federal law should serve only to mediate the selling and parceling out of a debtor's assets to his creditors.

Within two years of the law's passage in August 1898, 40,000 people filed for voluntary bankruptcy and between $600 and $700 million in debts were discharged. For one bankrupt, the feeling of relief from a court settlement was enthusiastically shared with a journalist as he emerged from a courtroom: "This is the first free breath I have drawn in a decade."[16] Out of a total of 24,000 bankrupts discharged of their debts, one-half were wage earners, 10,000 were merchants, 1,000 were manufacturers, and another 1,000 were from the professions.[17] The discriminatory rule of law that once pitted the man of business or trader against the ordinary citizen, and the citizen against the corporation, had forever vanished.

For one hundred years, the nation had debated. Again and again its legislators experimented with bankruptcy laws, only to be struck down repeatedly by regional interests. These would ultimately be submerged by deep-rooted changes in the economy of a fast-growing nation. Many of the nation's most enlightened and famed leaders had spoken out on the question of rights and responsibilities that matched debtor against creditor. One of the more profound insights was voiced by Henry Clay in April 1840. The message still rings true.

> The right of the State to the use of the unimpaired faculties of its citizens as producers, as consumers, and as defenders of the Commonwealth, is paramount to any rights or relations which can be created between citizen and citizen. . . . I maintain that the public right of the State in all the faculties of its members, moral and physical, is paramount to any supposed rights which appertain to a private creditor. This is the great principle which lies at the bottom of all bankrupt laws.

This view is encompassed in a belief—now codified—that the debtor in trouble has a right to a second chance. It gave the bankrupt a new lease on life. Rules encompassing this belief are commonly known as the rehabilitation clauses of modern bankruptcy law. While their origins can be found in the French trading ordinances of the seventeenth century, they had taken two hundred years to take root and germinate into legislated language. The main theme of such experimental legal seedings was that once a majority of creditors had agreed to a settlement, the result would be binding on all others. This novel process in effect wiped the debtor's slate clean and allowed him to emerge free from the possible claims of a dissenting minority of creditors. This feature is now recognized by most nations as a cornerstone of the economic utility of bankruptcy law. Such measures allowed settlements to occur without terminating the productive life of a debtor by liquidating his assets and provided the basis for planning a new lease on life.

THE TECHNICALITIES OF BANKRUPTCY LAW

Legal jurisdiction over bankruptcy is in the hands of federal courts. Appeals move in two stages upward to the federal court of appeals and to the Supreme Court.

Two kinds of bankruptcy are allowed. One is voluntary, allowing the debtor to take the initiative to petition for a discharge of debts; the other is involuntary and is initiated by three or more creditors if there are more than twelve, or by a single creditor if less than twelve.

Distinctions are made between bankruptcy and insolvency. The former applies to cases in which a debtor does not have enough money or assets to pay debts. Insolvency, on the other hand, can refer to a debtor's inability to pay debts as they come due and may not always imply actual bankruptcy.

******

In 1898, the Torrey Bankruptcy Bill was passed. It was drafted in several chapters. The first provided definition of terms, the second established a court system, the third defined eligibility for bankruptcy, the fourth focused on court procedures, the fifth created a system of trustees and referees in bankruptcy proceedings, the sixth called for meetings between creditors and the bankrupt.

In 1938, the act was subtantially amended to include specific provisions for corporations and individuals. Four new chapters appeared. Chapter X—Corporate Reorganizations, allowing a corporation to propose a method of reorganizing itself back into financial health; Chapter XI—Arrangements, allowing corporations to enter into settlement agreements with creditors; Chapter XII—Real Property Arrangements by Persons other than Corporations; Chapter XIII—Wage Earner's Plans.

In 1978, these new chapters were greatly simplified in another major amendment of the original Torrey Bankruptcy Act. Arabic numerals were substituted for Roman Chapter numbers, and chapters X, XI, and XII were consolidated into a single Chapter 11 business reorganization program. Individuals were covered under a revised Chapter 13. The clear, basic language and broad substance of the 1898 Torrey Bill were left intact.

Chapter XI of the old act was originally designed for use by the the nonpublic small business. Chapter XI contained a faster procedure for an arrangement of the debtor's unsecured debt, but the secured debt structure could not be altered. Chapter 11 of the new code attempts to combine the completeness of Chapter X with the speed and greater flexibility of Chapter XI.

"Proceedings under Chapter 11 are designated as reorganizations, and are available to all who are eligible for liquidation proceedings as discussed above, except stockholders and commodity brokers, and railroads, and may affect the rights of all creditors, secured or unsecured, and stockholders as well. The purpose of a business reorganization case, unlike a liquidation case, is to restructure the finances of a business so that it may continue to operate, pay creditors and produce a return for its stockholders. The purpose of a reorganization or arrangement case for a debtor is to formulate, and have confirmed, a reorganization plan so that it can continue in business."[18]

Under the new laws, a debtor seeking court protection is given four months to come up with a recovery plan. One half the creditors representing at least two-thirds of the debt must approve within 180 days—a difficult problem for the debtor to negotiate while trying to save an ailing operation. If agreement cannot be reached the creditors can take the initiative to recommend a plan.

Current reform initiatives are focused on a tightening of terms affecting individuals filing for bankruptcy. A rapid rise in the rate of individuals filing after the 1978 amendment is viewed by many as a result of an overly liberalized code.

What this legal evolution does not tell us, though, is how to control the indebtedness of what I have labeled the "new bankrupts"—giant publicly held corporations, local governments as big as New York City or the state of Michigan, and nations as large as Brazil or as mismanaged as Poland. The new bankrupts bring with them a new set of problems requiring new solutions and innovative applications of the two fundamental contributions of our evolved bankruptcy laws: the right to a second chance and the settlement of debt for less than its face value. We turn now to the new bankrupts and the problems they bring, a legacy of the financiers' decade.

Chapter 3

CORPORATE GIANTS

The collapse of the Penn Central raised questions about conglomerates and diversification programs; about the role of boards of directors and how they function, or failed to function; about the inherent conflicts of interest that arise as a result of incestuous, interlocking directorates between financiers who supply money, managers who borrow the money, and brokers who traffic with both; about the relationship between big government and big business. And about the condition of American capitalism.

Daughen & Binzen, *The Wreck of the Penn Central*

IT HAPPENED on June 21, 1970. Since then, things have not quite been the same in America. That day marked the historic and unparalleled Penn Central crash and declaration of bankruptcy. Except for collapses caused by fraudulent practices, no firm in the United States with assets any larger than $25 million had ever gone bankrupt. If only because of the sheer size of Penn Central, an ignominious precedent was set. Within weeks, the collapse of this conglomerate giant affected almost 100,000 employees, 186 subsidiary companies involved in everything from railroads to basketball teams, 100,000 creditors, 118,000 stockholders, and a yearly volume of business in excess of $4.5 billion.

The day it filed for reorganization, the company cash balance totaled a paltry $7,308,130; its current liabilities of about $750 million exceeded its current assets by about $280 million. The accumulated liabilities of the Penn Central Transportation Co., totaled an unbelievable $3.6 billion; its parent holding company, the Penn Central Co., held another $125 million of obligations. In 1982 dollars the giant owed a cumulative equivalent of $9.1 billion and had no means to pay it. In the waning weeks of its life a

29

sudden disappearance of $4 million is said to have finally tipped the balance. An international businessman from Liechtenstein, Alfred J. Bühler, would be implicated. Efforts to pursue him and others implicated with him were blocked by the intercession of the Central Intelligence Agency.[1]

All that might have been wrong with accounting procedures, an incestuous and clubby board of directors, an investor community wooed by a well-crafted public relations facade, an overconfident banking community, and an incompetent management team came to a head in 1970—only two years after its successful conclusion of the largest agglomerated corporate merger ever in the United States.

Penn Central's insolvency filing under Section 77 of the Bankruptcy Act, written specifically to cover railroad failures, touched almost every significant bank in the nation; it almost prevented the U.S. Department of Transportation from finding knowledgeable legal counsel because so many had direct or tangential ties to the tentacular net of interests held by the parent Penn Central Co. This was the railroad that controlled so diverse a portfolio that no corporate executive could identify its entire panoply of holdings. It was also the one whose three key executives at the helm during its last years were so caught up in their own egocentricities that they were no longer able to work together and assiduously avoided contact with one another.

This was the company that while losing money at a rate of $1 million a day in the first quarter of 1970, and owing in excess of $1.5 billion in long-term debts and another $300 million in revolving credit, still had to contend with almost $200 million in commercial paper due by year's end. Its interest payments alone for the year were estimated at $130 million.

Despite all, its finance chairman, David Bevan, was able to paper over the obvious ill-starred performance and woo the financial community into considering a new $100 million debenture to pay off part of the coming debt payments. He wasn't quick enough, though, to hide the first-quarter income statements for 1970. In three months losses had accumulated to over $100 million—twice as much as forecast, in part because of a lengthy and crippling snowstorm. Compounding Bevan's problems was a collapse in the stock worth of a real estate holding company through which future borrowing was being leveraged. From a peak of almost $1 billion in pyramided paper worth, the Great Southwest Corporation (owned by the Pennsylvania Company and in turn by the Penn Central Co.) toppled to a mere $50 million.

The seams were unraveling and they soon tore apart. An almost blindly faithful financial community made a sudden about-face with an outspoken loss of confidence in the 122-year-old institution and its unblemished record of paying dividends for every one of those years. Why the pain had endured this long without any earlier attempts at drastic surgery was partially described in findings of the House Committee on Banking and Currency: "Every aspect of the issues involved in the collapse of the corporation appears to lead back to some banking institution." It disclosed that sixteen out of twenty-three Penn Central directors were members of bank boards; they collectively held twenty-four directorships in those banks. The committee queried: "Which interests were directors of the Penn Central representing in negotiating such loan agreements when they were also connected with the banking institutions lending money to the railroad?"[2]

Insider information and the bad news from the latest quarterly statements hit the marketplace. In a binge of stock selling, more than a quarter of the outstanding stock turned over during May 1970. Stocks valued at $86 a share in 1968 were now selling for $10.

Penn Central finally fell over the brink when the federal government, following President Richard Nixon's instructions, refused to honor twenty-fifth-hour loan guarantee agreements negotiated by transportation secretary John Volpe, much to the latter's embarrassment. Heading for a reelection, Nixon had seen the ripe opening for a hot political scandal—and he turned against an inner club of business supporters cum public servant friends. The secretary of the treasury, David Kennedy, also involved in the negotiations, had been president of the Continental Illinois Bank & Trust Company which had $15 million in loans to the Penn Central. Maurice Stans, Secretary of Commerce, and Walter

Annenberg, Ambassador to England, had direct financial interests in Penn Central holdings. Also, Randolph Guthrie, Nixon's former law partner, was retained to help the company in its representations to the federal government. Once again, the ethical conflicts between two-hatted and three-hatted roles became evident as word spread of links between the ambassador and the cabinet officers to the Penn Central. The crisis of its collapse raised new questions about the relationship of a private industry of basic importance to the well-being of the national economy and the political leadership elected to protect the public interest.

The failure was like a dam bursting. It opened a breach that was never to be fully blocked again and through which a flood of other giants surged during the ensuing decade, some to reemerge years later dressed in new clothes and with new corporate portfolios. Penn Central Co., for example, resurfaced eight years after its bankruptcy as the Penn Central Corp.; the notorious Equity Funding metamorphosed in three years into the Orion Capital Corp. Others, like the giant W. T. Grant, were liquidated and simply died.

What Goes Wrong

Statistics compiled by Dunn and Bradstreet on corporate failures in the United States indicate that more than 90 percent are a result of mismanagement or inexperience. In many cases warning signs that should have been exposed for directors and shareholders to see lay buried either through incompetence or through the overt efforts of vulnerable managers.

What happened to the giant chain store W.T. Grant offers ample testimony to how poorly management can perform. The outside world looked for and saw one thing; the real inside picture—antiquated accounting procedures and poor management practices—was shielded from view. In restrospect, some analysts think that the company was broke eight years before it declared itself bankrupt, despite a bullish performance of its earnings and stock performance until two years before its demise.

The corporation, in operation for sixty-nine years, employed about 80,000 people in a network of 1,200 stores nationwide. Through 1973 it never diverged from reporting profits or paying dividends. Yet, in just a few years, *short-term* debt had spiraled upward from almost none in 1969 to $600 million by the end of 1975; long-term debt curved sharply upward from $32 million in 1971 to $216 million four years later. The numbers reflected a strategic decision taken in the early 1960s to expand the number and size of its stores; to enlarge the variety of products sold and become a "full-line" store as others had already successfully become; to lease new sites away—yes *away*—from the growing main regional suburban shopping centers and in marginally profitable urban commercial strips; and, perhaps most critically, to promote new customer credit sales heavily—in the view of some observers, the Achilles heel of its efforts.

Not only did W. T. Grant borrow heavily for marginally profitable purposes but it decided at the very same time to lend money to its customers on unusually liberal terms. In one strategic step it became not only a debtor but also a creditor. To its customers, the company offered an old idea. They could buy a coupon book on credit and pay for it in small monthly install-ments. In the interim coupons could be redeemed for goods. The problem that ultimately undid the company was its credit account-ing method and the effect it had on corporate cash flow—the difference between the cost of doing business and the amount of money taken in. W. T. Grant reported to its shareholders as income the money and interest due from its coupons *before* it was actually paid; to the Internal Revenue Service it said that what it told its shareholders didn't apply and only the *actual* amount received was income for tax purposes. The external appearance was evident: that of a successful and healthy retail giant. This image stuck until 1973. It survived in large part by a rapid surge in the debt obligations of the company. This borrowed money helped to maintain the company's dividends policy and shored up its illusory profitability for several years.

An edifice of false fronts was being built that escaped the attention of shareholders and unattentive directors until too late.

Other factors soon conspired in accelerating the demise. A downturn in the economy, poorly monitored inventory, faulty store locations inspired by widely rumored real estate kickbacks to corporate executives, and a weak central management unleashed the inevitable. By 1974, the company auditors, Ernst and Ernst, acknowledged the illusory accounting game and suggested a probable back-tax burden to the IRS of a debilitating $51 million.

In the world of business, one hears the seemingly wisest investors and analysts using earnings per share as the true measure of company's standing. If anything was learned from the W. T. Grant collapse it was that, as a business magazine wrote, "a mask of profitability can easily be superimposed upon a mess of insolvency."[3] By coincidence, in 1974, the year that Grant was baring its financial soul on Wall Street, the Harvard School of Business Administration was experimenting with a new course in its first-year finance class. The buzzword that year was "funds flow" and the intent was to strip away decades of accounting obfuscation and come to the true bottom line of a company's performance: cash flow. Traditional methods, generally known as the Generally Accepted Accounting Procedures (GAAP), had long clouded this litmus test by adding annual depreciation figures to earnings to get at an inflated picture of the actual cash flow. This proved well and fine as long as the rate of inflation remained steady from year to year. But as soon as inflation—following in the wake of the Vietnam war economy—escalated upward, last year's depreciation no longer could be compared to this year's more expensive replacement costs for the depreciated equipment or plant being written off. The effect was to overstate earnings and to understate the future cost of replacing plant and equipment from corporate cash flow.

The new funds flow analysis got right down to the basics. It pointed the finger at the true change in corporate cash resources from year to year. Interestingly, while many companies now use funds flow analysis in their financial statements, the business school dropped the experimental course in favor of going back to teaching the older GAAP—which ironically creates a genuine 'gap' by insulating illusion from reality.

SAXON—"An accounting scandal ..."

April 15, 1982. Following a decade of profitable operations, Saxon Industries, a $700 million a year manufacturer of paper, business products, and copying machines, surprised the investment community by unexpectedly filing for bankruptcy.

To one of the company's board members and largest shareholder, Hal Kroeger, the filing "is a scandal—the kind of thing that shouldn't be allowed to happen in an American corporation. This has been a massive elaborate fraud."[4] The problem was a sudden disclosure by corporate officials that 1981 would end not just at loss, or the $24 million they predicted, but at $47 million—an amount escalated by nonexistent inventory of copying machines and paper. Alarmed creditors, including a number of banks holding $140 million in loans outstanding, quickly organized to investigate the firm's accounting procedures; so did the Securities and Exchange Commission.

One accounting game uncovered, not uncommon in many equipment-manufacturing and leasing firms, involved selling a copying machine to one client and finding a second client to lease it. Saxon acted as the intermediary, collecting lease payments and servicing the equipment. What it failed to do, however, was to note the obligation to pay the new owner as a liability on its balance sheet. The effect was to fraudulently alter the true appearance of the company's financial health.

Concerned about the need to create a better analytical tool to overcome old accounting methods, an investment firm—Kidder, Peabody, & Co.—invented something it labeled discretionary cash flow. It applied the new label to all cash that was left over after a company paid for the maintenance of its equipment, plant, and dividends. The remaining cash was the amount that could be used at its discretion to finance growth—clearly an amount a serious investor would want to know about. To Kidder, Peabody's amazement this new tool produced some unexpected results. It compared two companies, Dow Chemical and Union Carbide, that had impressive earnings records for a period from 1976 to 1979. Their records showed accumulated earnings of $2.5 billion and $1.8 billion respectively. But when the discretionary cash flow measure was applied the results showed a healthy Dow Chemical with almost $1 billion available to it and a Union Carbide with a *negative* discretionary flow of minus $663 million. By forgoing capital investment to maintain or replace plant and equipment, it

35

was in effect borrowing from itself to maintain a healthy posture in the eyes of its shareholder constituents.

Kidder, Peabody, & Co.'s analysis, published in *Forbes* magazine in early 1981,[5] compared two-thirds of the companies used to determine the Dow Jones Average. One-half these companies showed negative discretionary cash flow.

A comparison of General Motors and IBM illustrated the extreme case to which the shell game of corporate balance sheets can be put. From 1975 to 1979, General Motors accumulated $2.1 in negative discretionary cash while IBM had amassed a large positive discretionary pool of $11 billion; in 1980 alone, GM's negative total had increased by $4.9 billion while IBM added another $3.4 billion to its discretionary fund. Some one-time star companies on the "negative" list included obvious ones like Bethlehem Steel and U.S. Steel; some unexpectedly poor performers included International Harvester, Sears Roebuck, and Du Pont. The discretionary measure may seem logical and vital to the investor, but within the relatively incestuous accounting world there remains little agreement on how to standardize accounting principles to come to a true measure of a company's stability and performance.

From such corporate earnings reports a principal lesson can be learned. Such figures identify corporate profitability *on paper;* true cash flow, on the other hand, reflects the actual pulse. A reminder of the fickleness of numbers is that 1976 was a banner year for profitability at the Chrysler Corporation—a year during which large performance bonuses were paid to its key executives. A year later it went begging to Washington for a $1 billion bailout at the taxpayer's risk.

By 1981, the fragility of giant corporations grew more evident. The chairman of New York University's M.B.A. program, Professor Edward I. Altman, estimated that 10 percent of the nation's leading 2,000 companies show signs of distress.[6] But if Penn Central and W. T. Grant failed because managerial mistakes were made, others, like Wickes Cos., fell victim to external events that laid bare overzealous decisions to expand through cash-costly acquisition. When Wickes filed for bankruptcy protection under Chapter 11 of the Bankruptcy Act, it joined the ranks of the largest recorded failures in the United States. Its liabilities totaled more than $2 billion in April 1982. One hundred thousand stockholders and 15,000 creditors had interests at stake.

As a giant in the lumber and furniture industry, it suffered from both a plunge in housing construction and the surging cost of debt it incurred to finance its growth through acquisitions. The news tumbled the value of its shares from $17 to $3.9. The company is now fighting to recover under the tutelage of a turnaround specialist, Sanford C. Sigoloff. At risk are $580 million in short-term loans from banks, much of it supplied by a group of sixteen banks in the United States, Canada, and Europe. One of the first victims on Sigoloff's recovery efforts was the $300 million a year Wickes subsidiary, Aldens, Inc., a mail-order catalog operation. This partial collapse sacrificed 2,600 jobs, most of which were held by lifelong employees.

While Wickes Cos. may be attempting to get its house in order on its own terms—at least in the opening rounds, this luxury is less and less common to other firms in financial difficulty. A tough stance by worried bankers forced the giant White Motor Corp. into bankruptcy in 1980 by pushing for increased collateral to support portions of an accumulated $730 million in liabilities. Unable to cover $77 million in short-term debt due to twenty-seven banks, Chapter 11 filing was resorted to—but not in time to protect deposits seized by two banks holding company cash. Employees in Cleveland, whose checks bounced because of the unexpected seizure, had to be issued checks on an account in a distant small-town bank far from the clutches of the city's banks.

White's ills traced back to excessive inventories of heavy-duty trucks that the 1975 recession left sitting in company storage lots. A similar fate affected its tractor division as farm sales lagged in subsequent years. And despite a highly profitable credit subsidiary, White Motor Credit, the $1.2 billion a year company could not survive the pressures of declining sales of its trucks and tractors, both of which were felt to be ineffective dollar-for-dollar competitors with rival products. Its woes, brewing for several years, were brought to a head by the recalcitrance of its creditor banks.

The lessons learned by a toughened banking community were applied with added vigor to the feverish $6 billion equipment manufacturer, International Harvester, the third-largest construction equipment manufacturer in the world (behind Caterpillar & Komatsu (Japan) in size). It gained the dubious reputation of posting the largest single loss of any American corporation in one fiscal quarter: $1 billion, an amount larger than total sales for that same period.

In Harvester's case a consortium of 225 banks banded together in 1981 to set the terms for a huge $4.9 billion refinancing agreement. The outcome, while pleasing to the banks, may prove hollow. Commenting on the unusually tight controls imposed by the banks, *Business Week* wrote about the three-year reorganization plan: "Until 1984, Harvester will essentially be working for the banks, whose short-term demands seriously conflict with the company's long-term needs."[7] One of the terms imposed on the company was that no new major capital investments be made despite a $500 million a year requirement estimated as necessary to keep pace with competitors. Quoting a banker immersed in the firm's activities, the same magazine wrote: "We've been trying to change a big company mentality, in which management thinks it can do as it pleases, to an outlook that 'we're really in trouble; now what can we do about it?'"

The International Harvester case points to another problem area in the mores of doing business in America: conflict of interest—in this case between the operating business and the banks that supply its financing. One of the firm's board members, the chairman of the Continental Illinois National Bank & Trust Co., Roger E. Anderson, allowed himself to play out two irreconcilable roles, one as an individual mandated to promote the interests of a manufacturing firm, the other to protect a loan of $200 million issued by his bank. The evident conflict led to his resignation from the International Harvester board in early 1981. Such conflicts, not uncommon on the boards of many U.S. public and private corporations, were put to the test by a growing consensus among bankers that an economic cycle of high interest rates and a recessionary marketplace required tough new lending standards. This new understanding is helping to redefine the ethics of the friendly banker on the corporate board. As the stakes have grown to threaten huge conglomerates with complex and large financing burdens, the role of the bankers has become more adversarial than cuddling.

The failure of the Penn Square Bank in Oklahoma City in July 1982 left the same Continental Illinois Bank of Chicago reeling with more than $1 billion in related loan liabilities. While clouded in fraudulence, the Penn Square affair was in large part a creature of a financial community riding on the last crest of easy-to-give, easy-to-get credit. Collateral, as fragile as boardroom promises of a producing oil well, could leverage immense amounts of money. According to the *Tulsa Tribune,* Kenneth E. Tureaud, a former football star at the University of Michigan, received a $30 million loan from the bank. Collateral to secure this loan was provided with spurious oil and gas leases on which there was no clear title. And despite statutory credit limits of $3.5 million to any single party associated with the bank, a director, Carl W. Swan, was able to amass $200 million in loans from Penn Square for his business interests.[8] The effects of such worthless loans quickly leapfrogged to the nation's third-largest banking institution, the Chase Manhattan Corporation, which was forced to post an unprecedented loss in its second-quarter earnings.

Continental Illinois chairman Roger E. Anderson sought to divert the critical publicity glare by announcing, unconvincingly,[9] that he was satisfied with his lending strategy but that new controls and procedures were being reviewed. In December the head of a new credit risk evaluation division was appointed with the intention of applying a credit rating method similar to that used by the U.S. Comptroller of the Currency. Such belated face saving could not hide an immense inventory of poorly monitored loan decisions by that one bank and the implicit acknowledgment of an inferior loan operation. This revealed decisions to help bankroll an almost complete list of the nation's major bankruptcy cases as well as individuals on the rebound from earlier failures such as Richard L. Burns, the founder of R.L. Burns Corporation and later chairman of Nucorp Energy Inc., an oil exploration supplies conglomerate. Nucorp filed for bankruptcy protection in July 1982 with $525 million in debt—almost a third of which is owed to Continental of Illinois and its subsidiaries.

Looking back to June 22, 1970, one can now see the writing of a new chapter in American corporate history. Penn Central became the first of many cases that tested an ephemeral cement that gives stability to a capitalist economy—investor confidence. Trust, perhaps the single most important factor in sustaining the bond between lender and borrower, would erode in the ensuing years. Shareholders would question the competence of those entrusted to manage the performance of the assets they own, holders of debt would challenge the integrity of the institutions that issue the "paper" commitment to honor the terms of the debt, and most participants in the economic mainstream—from employees to managers to investors—would start to question the ability of government to maintain the credibility of a nation's currency and debt. In the 1970s and with a quickened pace in the first years of the 1980s, that erosion was not reversed.

Some of the most evident causes for alarm, such as the pervasive and damaging effects of the energy crisis or the rising tide of economic protectionism affecting world trade, could not hide a new, and more readily curable, realization. Many of the causes of failures in giant corporations—commonly believed to be more immune to distress than smaller and younger firms—are attributed to bad judgment, mismanagement, fraudulent behavior, and a basic disregard for the public responsibility vested in corporate management and the board of directors.

That directors held a singular responsibility to the employees, shareholders, customers, suppliers, and the general public long escaped legal definition. But in August 1982, a little-noticed case signaled a major shift in court attitudes toward the responsibility of directors in bankruptcy cases. The U.S. District Court for the Southern District of New York held a director of a bankrupt firm, the Newfoundland Refining Co. (NRC), personally liable for $11 million because of company loans of $30 million made to NRC's sole shareholder and owner during two years prior to the company's collapse.[10] The decision, challenged by the defendant, was upheld in the U.S. Second Circuit Court of Appeals. Roy Furmark, the former director of the NRC, argued in vain that the decision against him had disastrous implications for corporate directors.

Penn Central may have succumbed to self-inflicted ossification. In restrospect, though, the blindness of its board to the depth of its growing ills and the decadence of its managerial culture allowed the mushrooming conglomerate to attempt survival through diversification. The decision was ill fated from the start given the enormity of the problem caused by the failing railroad operations. So too, perhaps, for W. T. Grant and a multitude of others whose mismanagement only delayed and aggravated the looming crisis of bankruptcy. The ultimate tragedy is that their failures extracted a price from those least able to protect their interests: the employees, whose lives are dislocated; the shareholders, whose assets are rendered valueless; and the community, whose welfare is linked to the health of the corporate employer. These failures argued for a more strenuous oversight mechanism, in particular where the interests of shareholders and employees were at stake without adequate representation. The need for a process to trigger emergency measures in response to the mismanagement or even fraudulent actions of corporate directors, bank lending officers, and corporate officers seems more necessary than ever as the threat of billion-dollar collapses looms larger and larger.

But what came to shock America even more during the unsettling 1970s was the sudden and disarming discovery that government itself was as fragile as industry. The bankruptcy of the nation's second-largest government shook the political and economic environment with far greater impact than was felt in the Penn Central demise.

Chapter 4

WE'RE SOLID
AND STRONG

THE LESSONS learned in accounting and finance departments of large corporations were not lost on the public sector. Many local governments, particularly cities, pressed by their constituents to provide a widening array of services and by their employees to provide higher salaries and benefits, learned quickly the creative arts of the financier.

Some of the most innovative borrowing practices emerged in the back-room dealings of public officials faced with annual budgets that leapfrogged local revenue capacities. Reaching into the till of debt in ever larger and ever more creative ways became a modern art of public finance. It would be in New York City that the art of public indebtness reached its peak. What emerged was an unbelievable Rube Goldberg debt structure cemented together by equal doses of reality, illusion, and accounting magic.

When the city ran out of money in 1975, the outcome reverberated for years. In its wake, the public soon discovered an embarrassing array of back-scratching arrangements between city officials and the nation's leading lending institutions. The methods and ethics of bank lending habits to New York City would be called into question by the Securities and Exchange Commission (SEC). The SEC's concerns focused on irresponsible and misleading representation of securities issued to the general public on behalf of the city.

For those on the outside looking in, the discoveries were alarming. As budget director of the state of New York during the city's and the state's crisis years, Peter Goldmark was a participant in the struggle to reestablish the integrity of the nation's second-largest government. Now director of the Port Authority of New York with offices on the sixty-seventh floor of the World Trade Center, it is fitting that he looks out on a vast panorama of the metropolis whose financial future he helped remold. Beside him is a framed quotation taken from the ancient Oath of Athenian State. "We will ever strive for the ideals and sacred things of the city . . .

"The debt of municipal governments," he said, "is one of the great uncharted and unregulated areas of American finance." And he added, "there's an astonishing lack of knowledge on how it works."[1] This had not always been so. During the 1950s and before, the borrowing ground rules were relatively straightforward and the debt capacity of public institutions was easy to measure. If a local government needed to borrow one could quickly establish whether or not it had the taxing or revenue capacity to bear the burden.

"This was a local government structure in which everyone knew their roles," Goldmark says. "The executives set priorities, the legislature raised taxes as needed, and the judiciary defined boundaries of conflicting claims. All this worked very well in an environment of no inflation and simple program demands." He termed this nirvana a "flat world" bounded only by fixed levels of expenses and a single revenue base of real property.

Rising consumer expectations during the 1960s would change all that. Not only did this result in the broadening of usable revenue sources, but additional financial commitments would be made on very fickle funding foundations. Inflation introduced an unanticipated volatility; the economic cycle turned more extreme in its peaks and valleys, thereby affecting tax revenues flows; and short-term fluctuations became more erratic. In many states the tax curve could move up or down radically within a single fiscal year. To meet rising expenditure pressures local authorities sought funds from a broader array of both state and federal government agencies.

One facet of the new business of public debt most dismaying to Goldmark was a growing permissiveness toward the quality of the security built into new indebtedness. He recalled one of the most creative inventions to occur in the financial world in a long time. "This was the John Mitchell [of Watergate fame] 'moral obligation bond.'" This innovation—instigated in part at the request of a New York governor hungry for construction money, Nelson Rockefeller—would later cause immense difficulties in the state by allowing debt obligations to be incurred without any public review or referendum. Thus vanished the "full faith" backing of public debt, to be replaced by a more innocuous "but we will make good" promise. By this mechanism any shortfalls in revenues required only that the budget director notify the legislature to appropriate the shortfall—and in effect meet its "moral obligation." A virtually limitless money machine was invented that could technically by-pass depression era laws that restricted commercial banks from underwriting revenue bonds. Mitchell's moral obligation formula let loose a binge of commercial banking participation in underwriting municipal and state debt. And not incidentally, observed Goldmark, this allowed banks to create a huge new business.

By the end of the 1960s, the blossoming business of financing city, regional transit, water, and school authority debts had become a world unto itself. All could go directly to the marketplace and buy debt at the going rate. "There were no overseers," says Goldmark. Thus the stage was set for the New York City calamity of 1975—in the judgment of many students of federal financing tactics, a looming national crisis.

Penn Central may have looked like a giant when it fell prey to mismanagement, yet it would look small next to the eventual financial collapse of the nation's largest city. New York City employed almost three times as many people as did Penn Central at its peak. The city's debt in 1975 was five times larger than the railroad conglomerate's bankruptcy liabilities. Nothing about America's largest city, the communications and banking nerve center of the national economy, was normal or typical in the mid-1970s. The richest and poorest, the biggest and the smallest, the best and worst—all the superlatives fit.

New York is a world city whose changing economy would leapfrog the institutions intended to serve the demands of a more traditional economic base. Over a thirty-year period, it lost jobs in almost every sector—construction, manufacturing, transportation, communications, utilities, wholesale trade, and retail trade. But those losses, while difficult to bear, signaled fundamental changes in the nature and structure of the city's urban economy. While its service, government, and finance-insurance-real estate sectors grew from a total of 1.2 million employed people to 1.9 million, its manufacturing base was reduced by almost half, to 500,000.

As the city changed, City Hall found itself steadily losing ground in keeping pace with a weakened economic base, a loss of middle-class taxpaying residents, and a steady influx of aliens dependent on public assistance. Solutions were found. Under Mayor John Lindsay and his successor Abraham Beame, the city comptroller from 1969 to 1973, numerous accounting tricks were used to keep the faltering ship afloat. The New York State Charter Commission, concerned about an inordinantly rapid rise in the city's short-term debt between 1969 and 1975, decided the central reason was

the City's refusal to soundly finance its expense budget. Since 1970-71, every expense budget has been balanced by an array of gimmicks—revenue accruals, capitalization of expenses, raiding reserves, appropriation of illusory fund balances, suspension of payments, carry-forward of deficits and questionable receivables, and finally the creation of a public benefit corporation whose purpose is to borrow funds to bail out the expense budget.[2]

One consultant found the city levying taxes on its own property in order to boost artificially the published revenue balances on one hand, and to permit borrowing against them on the other. He concluded his analysis with an estimate of bogus receivables exceeding $500 million. The effect was a fraudulently painted picture of the city's financial state of affairs in order to attract subscribers to new debt securities in the United States. The most damaging of what were labeled Ponzi-like shell games[3] was the use of the annual capital budget to pay for day-to-day expenses. As a result, within four years the capital budget quickly rose from $1 billion in 1970 to $2.2 billion, much of it financed by expensive debt. By 1981, the City Planning Commission would look back on this period by describing the shell game: "The City was able to finance a large part of the operations of its vocational high schools through the Capital Budget. Funding of such 'human capital projects'. . . . grew to as much as $750 million a year."[4] In its view, this was the primary contributing factor to the eventual crisis of 1975.

The problem was akin to a fixed-income household owner using expensive funds borrowed for a new roof to pay an unemployed cousin to mow the lawn. By the time the roof starts to leak his borrowing ability has evaporated and he is worse off than when he started. City planners calculated that after the 1975 financial crisis the deferred expenditures on vital repairs and construction were of disastrous proportions. The rate of street repairs was occurring once every 200 years; water mains once every 296 years. On the famed West Side Drive a car actually fell through the decayed roadbed. On the FDR East Side Drive concrete slabs fell from the ceilings of tunneled sections.

The city's comptroller, Harrison J. Goldin, would tell an audience of municipal and finance officers in May 1976, "there was a broad feeling, I believe, that even though the City's accounting and budgeting had been revealed as a kind of Rube Goldberg conception—a system which defied understanding or control—it was better to leave it alone as long as it churned out enough money to meet the bills and pay the debts."[5]

By March 1975, the city's outstanding debt was in excess of $14 billion, of which $6 billion was short term—one year or less. Annual debt service had risen to $1.8 billion and absorbed 16 percent of the budget; five years earlier the annual interest burden was almost a third smaller, at $675 million, and required only 10 percent of the budget. Under normal circumstances the city frequently borrowed short-term notes to finance gaps in meeting its long-term obligations. There was nothing unusual about this. Yet, what in better times was a financial safety valve now bloated out of proportion. Short-term notes were being issued to pay current expenses on the promise that they would be paid with future receipts from bond sales. When confronted later in the year by Felix Rohatyn on this spurious method, in particular because no one was buying the proposed bonds, First Deputy Mayor James Cavanagh answered: "I can see you don't know much about municipal financing." Rohatyn fired back: "Yes, but I know alot about baloney, and what you are giving me is just a lot of baloney."[6] The magnitude of the sham was immense. The city, with 3.2 percent of the nation's population, borrowed 20 percent of the total tax-exempt debt issued in the entire nation; by 1975 it was borrowing 30 percent of the total.[7] If federally guaranteed projects were excluded, New York's share of national short-term municipal debt jumped to 50 percent. Such concentrations of liability in a single institution meant only one thing: A bankruptcy would have resounding effects throughout the nation.

Yet, by a strange constitutional quirk, New York continued to retain high ratings for the quality of its debt. Early in 1975, while cities like Albany, Boston, Buffalo, and Pittsburgh were being downgraded to *B* ratings, New York held firm with its own *A* ratings. One reason was that the ratings services, such as Moody's and Standard & Poor's, focused far too narrowly on the gold-plated promise of the city's legal counsel that the state constitution makes debt service a priority charge on any collected public revenues. To a banker this meant being first in line for payment out of tax revenues; whether other obligations could be met was rarely considered of any relevance to the lending institutions. The money machine was working all too profitably. Meanwhile, for the city the deadline ticked toward a choice between paying for $1.5 billion in debt service or maintaining a bloated operating expense budget.

Time simply ran out. The state's capacity to help the city was exhausted. As the hands on the clock moved relentlessly toward the time for payment, emotions flared. New York fired away at Washington for not helping, and Washington chided back that New York could stew in its own financial morass. Federal Reserve Chairman Arthur Burns warned in May 1975 that any bank lending money to the city would open itself to shareholder suits for violating the "prudent man rule of investing."[8] Making matters worse, the seven largest city banks holding $1.25 billion worth of city notes in their portfolios and an estimated additional $1.75

billion in trust funds now refused to go any further in accepting new debt without drastic new austerity measures on the part of the city. In October, the *Daily News* printed the now infamous headline: "Ford to City: DROP DEAD"—a decision that may have cost the president a reelection victory by a narrow margin.

For all practical purposes New York City, America's most famed urban center and the world's financial capital, was bankrupt. One option was to file for bankruptcy under Chapter IX of the Bankruptcy Act reserved with astute foresight for local governments. That option was not resorted to. Looking back on the implications of a formal bankruptcy, Felix Rohatyn—who later helped engineer its recovery—recalls: "I rapidly came to feel that letting the city go down was inconceivable. Everybody would be lining up in front of a judge who didn't know what to do. Services would go to hell, and we would never be able to put things back together again."[9]

Confusion reigned. Even the simplest records of numbers of people employed could fluctuate by 50,000 from one week to the next, said Larry Kieves, now the deputy commissioner of the Office of Economic Development of New York City, who monitored the federal government's loan guarantees to the city as an employee of the U.S. Treasury Department. "The situation was chaotic," he recalled. "The word computer had not even been introduced into the comptroller's office."

While Mayor Abe Beame spun wheels on the city's financially ill-fated treadmill, in Albany matters were equally hectic. When Peter Goldmark entered his new office as budget director in 1975, he was far from aware of the tentacular fiscal nightmare into which he was stepping. "One of my first acts was to track holdings of all banks to determine what obligations the state, its special authorities, and the city owed or held. No one knew!" What resulted, he recalled, "was a wild atmosphere of eventually tracking and refinancing $20 billion in one year." In a final event of comic proportions, on the morning of March 12 a year later, the New York State police rounded up state assemblymen from bars, motels, and restaurants to ensure sufficient votes to keep the state out of default.

It was in the midst of this hectic period—punctuated by the failure of a Rockefeller invention, the Urban Development Corporation, to pay $105 million in notes due—that Abe Beame finally made his journey to plead his case in Albany. This was only six months after he had reportedly stated: "the City's credit position is 'solid and strong'. . . . There is absolutely no question about the City's ability to repay all its debts on time, and that this ability has improved over the last fifteen years."[10] In early April 1975, he asked for an appointment with Governor Hugh Carey and Peter Goldmark. To them His Honor announced: "We have $400 million coming due and no way to repay them." What he failed to mention—perhaps not wanting to comprehend the tangled web of city financing—was that by then the total accumulated short-term debt was in fact fifteen times larger, that is close to $6 billion.

Instead of a quick fix to help the pleading mayor, New York State Governor Carey announced the creation of a committee to advise the state on appropriate steps. One member on the committee was Felix Rohatyn of Lazard Frères & Company, an internationally famed investment banking firm. In a written flourish *Business Week* suggested the coming of "Batman wizardry to save Gotham."[11] The Municipal Assistance Corporation soon came to life destined for a rapid rise to fame and the coining of a new acronym in the language of financiers—the MAC. And a battle for federal support from President Gerald Ford, who preferred the easy ploy of holding out against any help for New York, was launched. Eventually, MAC became the sole authority through which new financing could be issued on behalf of the city. Federal guarantees were negotiated and, under Rohatyn's leadership a strict austerity program was initiated.

Three important lessons emerged from the saga of saving New York City. The first was related to the broad issue of oversight of public debt. As a result of intensive media coverage, it became evident to the nation not only that the city's finances were beyond the control of any higher authority but that what had been witnessed in New York was far from being a self-contained aberration. The nation began to look around and question state and local government finances and to find wide-ranging spending and borrowing excesses. A new awareness of the vast scope of unmonitored public activity stimulated new efforts to rein in the spreading tentacles of local government financing. Proposition 13 took hold in California; Proposition 2 1/2 in Massachusetts; Ronald Reagan was elected in part on promises of curbing government spending.

A second lesson would be an understanding of the manipulations of short-term financial quick fixes at the expense of long-term needs. The expedient of paying immediate expenses by milking capital improvement debt was challenged. The dubious promise of repayment of short-term debt used for day-to-day expenses with future bonds issues earmarked, theoretically, for long-term capital projects was undermining the physical capacity of the city to maintain services. The deferral of capital expenditures was a time bomb that finally exploded.

A new insight into the responsibility—or irresponsibility—of banks in cultivating and aggravating the crisis of New York came as another lesson. Had the banks' actions been motivated by a commitment to keep New York City afloat, or were they strictly motivated by the profitability of their loans with far too little concern for the credibility of the borrower? What made these emerging issues even more pertinent was the realization that, far from being an anomaly, New York City's woes were shared by many others, worldwide, with similar laxity in external monitoring of the lending habits of banks or borrowing credibility of debtors.

Restoring Credibility

It would take until October 1981, more than six years, to bring the city back to normalcy and to institute operational oversight standards. That month the city had its first clean audit in which all was accounted for within a balanced budget—one year earlier than the requirements set by the federal government under its guaranteed loan agreements. Employment by the city is pared down to just under 200,000—a drop of 90,000 jobs from a few years earlier—and another 10,000 jobs are to be eliminated by the end of 1984. With a clean bill of health the city moved back into

51

the debt markets. In Larry Kieves' words, "no city is now watched more closely. No other city has a level of reporting New York has. No other city is better organized to prepare data the veracity of which is unquestioned. The scrutiny is higher than anywhere else." With its accounting standards in sound shape and a marketplace once again responsive to its needs, the city announced its gradual displacement of MAC bonds as a primary borrowing source. Early in 1983, the mayor and his comptroller outlined a plan to sell $150 million in bonds within six months, another $400 million a year later, almost twice that in 1985, and $1.1 billion in 1986. The sudden increase would be coordinated with MAC's expiration of its power to sell bonds.

Ironically, the pressure on the city by federal Treasury authorities to bring its affairs into line is rarely used elsewhere. As far back as 1972, a federal Revenue Sharing Act passed under President Nixon required local government financial statements of acceptable standards to the Treasury Department. This condition has never been imposed.

But out of the federal bailout relationship with New York came the Emergency Finance Control Board (EFCB), a state fiscal monitoring group created, at federal insistence, by Governor Carey. With the advantage of having a large staff in place within the state comptroller's office, it became the federal government's eyes and ears over New York City. By 1978 the E (Emergency) rating was dropped and a new permanent oversight institution came of age in the state. At the same time a new division of responsibility evolved at the state level starting with the creation of a deputy assistant secretary for state and local finance. Under him were created an Office of New York City Finance, an Office of Municipal and State Finance, and an Office of State and Local Fiscal Responsibility. "This gave us," says Goldmark, "a totally new capacity to monitor and detect coming problems of a sort that didn't exist at the time of the '75 crisis."

A Deferred Future

An awareness of an "indebted and decaying" America would be awakened by the potholes, rusting bridges, and leaky water mains of New York City's insolvent government. The method gone awry, in Felix Rohatyn's view, had a very simple ring to it. "Dont' tax—borrow. Taxation is painful. Whatever you don't have to do today, do tomorrow, or, preferably, after the next election." The ignored New York infrastructure of sewers, water pipes, roads and bridges, buildings, and services would soon be seen as only the tip of a national iceberg of monumental proportions. Yet, at a time when the Reagan administration argues for a military program costing in excess of $1.6 trillion of borrowed "deficit" money, it ignores the fact that national security also depends on a sound and working economic infrastructure. The price of reversing what *Newsweek* labeled "the decaying of America"[12] is estimated by some at a conservative $750 billion over the next seven years. Yet, the budgetary allocation to meet this need is almost nil.

What New York City demonstrated in its own crisis was the widely practiced propensity to defer repairs and capital expenditures in favor of current expenses. Politically, this tactic works as long as snow is removed and not too many potholes are seen. The problem confronts us when highways begin to crumble and fresh water feeds drainage ditches more rapidly than waterlines to homes, offices, and factories. Because the problem is national—and critical in its scale—it requires a federal solution. However, even at the federal level, there is no such thing as a domestic capital budget similar in character to a military budget. By this default of a policy mechanism one finds an abdication of federal responsibility to set the budgetary priorities required to reverse a decaying national infrastructure.

The Banker's Responsibility

Another outcome of the New York fiscal crisis was the suggestion that lending institutions took an active part in the creation of the fiscal crisis. It did not take long after 1975 for the federal Securities and Exchange Commission to issue a report that detailed events between October 1974 and April 1975, when in its words, "New York City faced a fiscal crisis and issued large amounts of short-term securities."[13]

53

The concern on which the commission focused was the issuance of $4 billion in short-term securities to thousands of small investors during the six months prior to the city's financial collapse in April. The commission determined that these investors had received less than a full and fair picture of the risks as a result of actions that involved "city officials, bond counsel, the underwriters of the City's securities, rating service officials and certain other persons. . . . Failure to make meaningful disclosure prolonged the agony of the City's fiscal crisis [and] caused undue risks and substantial injury to investors in the City's securities."[14]

As late as December, Standard & Poor's and Moody's rating services were issuing *A* standards for New York City Bonds. This remained in effect until April 2, when Standard & Poor's suspended the *A* rating; Moody's continued in its bullish evaluation by stating "the strong legal backing of the City's obligations and the City's unique position in the American economy provide a considerable amount of assurance to the creditor."[15]

In its report the commission recognized that the underwriters—Chase Manhattan Bank; First National City Bank; Morgan Guaranty Trust Company of New York; Manufacturers Hanover Trust Company; Bankers Trust Company; Merrill Lynch; Pierce, Fenner & Smith, Inc.; Weeden & Co.; and the Chemical Bank—were in a difficult position. They lived on a shaky tightrope between the responsibility to disclose fully how precarious the city's credit had indeed become and the duty to help support the city by providing continued credit. But in the commission's judgment "whatever reasons led the underwriters to market the City's securities without adequate disclosure, their conduct cannot be justified under the federal securities laws."[16]

Most damaging to the reputation and integrity of the underwriters was their early realization that they had saturated the normal marketplace for New York City securities during these final months. This concern led them to agree to a lowering of the denominations of the offerings. In a memorandum justifying such a step Merrill Lynch argued: "With $10,000 multiples. . . . this should open up a whole new market of potential tax-exempt note buyers. This should afford a great opportunity to open up new accounts and to bring in new funds."[17]

Adding to the lack of responsibility was that none of the underwriter banks, except Chemical, made any effort to retain portions of the offerings within their own portfolios as would normally be the case. In short, they were saying "pawn the risk off" on the small investor. In December Merrill Lynch, under a headline "Opportunity Knocks", urged its salesmen to look for the smaller investor. "Do your customers a favor," the firm admonished, "these notes are double-barrelled obligations and will be at very attractive yields." A few days later, with a devious appeal to its sales force, it circulated another directive: "Why not make some calls this evening and discuss New York City notes with your customers or prospects."[18] When interviewed later about their decision to buy these securities, many individual buyers referred to their broker's glowing reports of high ratings, first lien rights, and generally prudent investments.

The SEC found that many bonds were not merely improperly authorized but "illegally authorized." It reported the case of opinions issued by legal bond counsel—whose judgment determines the legality of a transaction in the eyes of the investor—that were far from candid. One firm, White & Case, discovered as late as March 1975 that the first lien guarantee of that month's offerings did not apply to the notes in question. "White & Case was aware of this information prior to the sale," reported the SEC commission. On March 14, $375 million in notes were offered. "However," said the SEC, "there was no disclosure of the first lien exception in connection with that offering."

Equally startling was the discovery by the commission that the underwriters' record keeping was sloppy at best. Bankers Trust kept typed ledgers but incomplete records of transactions. Chase maintained handwritten ledgers with trading transactions entered without explanatory notes. Many confirmations of trades were missing. Chemical maintained weekly computer records but also resorted to handwritten entries for trade-by-trade entries. Similarly, Citibank failed to maintain most of its confirmation records.

In many cases the bank could not locate records requested by the commission staff. Manufacturers Hanover did computerize all its entries but was found to be inaccurate in its monthly entry statements.

What the commission also uncovered from interviews with the underwriters was sadly inadequate research on the credit worthiness of clients as large and important as the city of New York. Each relied with undue trust on rating services and generally circulated information. At Merrill Lynch, prior to January 1975 no independent research was done. In its words, it "considered newspaper coverage relating to the City to be effective and comprehensive."

The behavior of the city, the banks, and the rating companies could not be condoned, the commission concluded. Their behavior "had the effect, at least in part, of shifting the risk of financing the City from the City's major banks and large institutional investors to individual investors."[19]

One constructive outcome of this unique period was most visible in the risk statements of underwriter companies. As Larry Kieves states: "Offering statements are far less blue sky than in 1975. Now you see risk factors stated in *worst case* terms." In a 1982 offering of $700 million, the 100-page background document contained two important statements. In bold letters on the opening page it warns: "The factors affecting the City's financial condition are complex. This Official Statement should be considered in its entirety. . . ." Later in its introductory remarks it points out that the "City now forecasts cash flow on a daily basis which has helped the City to improve its ability to project seasonal cash needs and to maximize its return on short-term investments." A new mood of fiscal responsibility had indeed been accelerated into life by the bankruptcy of the city in April 1975.

But if New York learned from its excesses, the lesson had yet to be applied by many others. Such mistakes, increasingly common in the United States, reached calamitous proportions abroad. Countries with a decade of accumulated debt many times larger than that of New York City began to steal the headlines starting in 1980. Poland was the first.

Chapter 5

A HOUSE OF CARDS

The OPEC situation led to an aberration, a permissive attitude towards borrowing. That couldn't go on forever, and that is what's happening. We're seeing the withdrawal symptoms.
David F. Lomax, *Group Economic Advisor, National Westminster Bank (London)*

All the great banks of the world have built a structure of debt that must surely be the largest and most remarkable financial house of cards ever created. It is still not clear how the governments, the central bankers and the great private bankers themselves could ever have believed that this structure would endure.
Harold Lever (Lord Lever of Manchester), *ex-cabinet minister under Prime Ministers Harold Wilson and James Callaghan.*

FOR A time Helmut Schmidt, West Germany's chancellor, saw himself as the Western world's leading statesman. During the 1970s his publicists would use his friendly rapprochement with Poland's Communist party chief, Edward Gierek, as evidence of a masterful grand plan to draw that nation out of Soviet clutches. The sweetened carrots in this grand plan were generous loans from German commercial banks. The money flowed freely and created such a bandwagon of interest that before long most of the industrialized world's leading lenders were joining in the perceived Polish economic miracle. But the miracle collapsed as fast as the Solidarity union movement was born, and with it was created one of the most extreme riches to rags stories of the postwar era.

Since Gierek's fall and Schmidt's shattered diplomatic initiatives, national indebtedness spread worldwide to become and

57

remain front page news. A principal reason is that many nations with economies as diverse as that of Poland to that of Brazil, Zaire, or Jamaica are in trouble. Heavy borrowers, most of these countries can no longer honor principal payments to lender banks and most are even hard put to meet inflation bloated interest payments. Adding to the crisis, unanticipated world events have aggravated the situation to a point of serious alarm. The oil price hikes of the mid-1970s, a world recession, unpredictable currency fluctuations, and the vulnerability of many one-commodity nations to market viscissitudes have conspired to erode confidence in national finance ministries and in world financial institutions. To many analysts the problem is of a global economic system in need of radical surgery.

For professionals whose business it is to monitor and evaluate the world of international finance, the crisis of debt is so complex and so diffuse that both generalizations and broad prescriptions of solutions are discouraged. At the World Bank, the director of economic analysis, Helen Hughes, argues that "there is no substitute for a thorough analysis of national economic management of debt." In her judgment, one can only understand the world debt problem on a nation by nation basis. To aggregate a discussion of the problem, and generalize the solutions to it, misses the point in her view. Optimistically, she feels that though the world faces immense debt problems, the proper policy prescription will make them manageable.

But even a comprehension of the unique, solvable dimension of a single country's problems should not detract from a studied appreciation of the broader, more global trends underlying them. Such a scan reveals some deeply etched weaknesses in the structure and performance of public and private international financial institutions.

While the world financial system itself was in part to blame for the crisis faced by a multitude of nations, the brinksmanship with bankruptcy in countries such as Poland—or its East Bloc comrade, Romania—was a wound largely self-inflicted by that nation's leaders with the support of Western bankers. Through administrative miscalculation and outright bungling and through the misjudgment of Western lending institutions, a country's economic vitality was sapped without a hint of concern by policymaker or lender until far too late. The parallel with New York City's own flirtation with bankruptcy was all too similar.

In 1982, Felix Rohatyn looked beyond American shores to an event as calamitous as the New York City crisis: the potential bankruptcy of a foreign government. He volunteered: "When New York teetered on the brink of insolvency in 1975—as Poland has been doing for months—many conservatives advocated that the city declare bankruptcy to symbolize the bankruptcy of liberalism carried to extremes. The symbolic lesson would have been devastating to both the city and New York State. A much stronger argument can be made that Poland should go bankrupt."[1]

The Polish dilemma held the unglamorous prospect of leaving Western banks with nearly $27 billion in unpaid debt aggregated over a decade. The U.S. share with interest due reached close to $4 billion. In July 1982, Treasury Secretary Donald T. Regan declared, "We don't want to do anything to upset the situation. We'll just leave the Polish debts outstanding and keep on talking." Such patience and flexibility hid within it two unavoidable realities. The first was the recognition that Poland was, for all practical purposes, bankrupt. The second was that public acknowledgment of this condition might force lender banks to write off immense sums as bad loans and thereby trigger a spiraling and unbearable financial crisis in the international lending community.

"Poland, Inc." is akin to a business enterprise that invented, and then actually used, a reverse gear to economic growth. In one year alone, from 1980 to 1981, its production of manufactured goods from shovels to trucks declined by 15 percent; its coal production, the mainstay of its economy and its key foreign currency earner, plunged from 200 million tons in 1980 to 162 million tons a year later. In three years, its GNP fell by a quarter. Stories of planning incompetence soon became legend. There is the tractor factory story, for example. One billion borrowed dollars were poured into creating a new tractor factory with a capacity of 75,000 units a year. Yet, when the production line opened it was able to produce at a rate of only 500 tractors a year.

To make matters worse for this unfortunate plant, the technology was purchased from the United States and not adapted to metric measures. As a result, the primary target market, neighboring Communist nations, failed to show any interest in buying the unserviceable machines.

Early in the 1970s, Poland was making commendable strides as a strong and seemingly healthy industrial economy. Its annual growth ran at a well-respected 7 to 8 percent a year. Its debt to Western banks and governments hovered around a manageable $1 billion. Imports and exports were well managed, one in equilibrium with the other. The nation, although one of the staunchest allies of the Warsaw Pact, was cultivating important political and economic collateral with the West. Germany's Helmut Schmidt was Party Secretary Edward Gierek's greatest promoter among the West European allies. In him, Schmidt saw the cement of a lasting alliance that might possibly help undermine East Germany's bond to Soviet Russia.

Rich in minerals, skilled labor, and a productive uncollectivized agricultural sector—85 percent of the cultivated land is privately owned—Poland was a successful, self-sufficient economy. Its biggest hopes lay in expanding its agricultural sector, building a stronger light industry base with its large pool of skilled workers, and exploiting its natural coal reserves. Instead, one of the centerpieces of the new Gierek economy was a $5 billion steel mill supplied by an equally costly rail line to ore sources in Russia. Once built, the mill never managed to produce steel in large enough volume to warrant the immense investment. Compounding the error was the impossibility of Poland's recovering its investment and meeting the mill's foreign debt because it could never expect to sell its steel for hard currencies on the world market at profitable prices.

The infamous Katowice mill and a long list of other ventures from tractors to television tubes shared two common failings. Most of them depended on foreign technology and parts to be built—all of which required huge sums of hard currency to finance purchases—and all depended on the successful re-export of end products to finance the original capital investments. The latter rarely materialized.

What Schmidt failed to see in time was a man launching his country on a self-destructive program of economic development. German banks would realize the implications far too late. Under Gierek's tutelage Poland was like a hot air balloon cut off from its heat source. Quite unglamorously, the economy deflated into the world's worst record of national decline since World War II. Within ten years its foreign debt grew twenty-five-fold, and it is expected to reach $33 billion by 1985; by 1981 imports exceeded exports at a rate of $1 billion a year, and annual growth was measured in negative figures.

Poland's problems were much like those of a child let loose in a toy shop with free use of a credit card. In this case, the toy shop offered a galaxy of glittering Western technologies available for the asking—all of them easily financed by Western bank loans. For Gierek and his planners the choices were irresistible. Their shopping list included everything that Poland was least prepared to use efficiently.

Quite unexpectedly, while many of the "modernizations" of the Polish economy were introduced by Gierek to appease violent unrest in 1970, they proved to be the fuel for even greater upheaval when the Gdansk Solidarity movement erupted in 1980 under Lech Walesa's magnetic leadership. The catalyst was rising meat prices in a country that could no longer pride itself in its ability to feed its own people. As more Polish hams went to foreign markets to pay for hard currency loans, fewer stayed home to feed Poles. Within months, the Gdansk shipyard revolt metamorphosed into a national movement of unparalleled proportion including nearly 10 million worker-members nationwide. A historic new era in Polish history had begun. Not only was the country financially bankrupted by Edward Gierek but it found itself ideologically bankrupt. The working class had turned against its ideological protector. The scale of the defection threatened the heart of Soviet-dominated Communist Europe.

Philippe de Weck, ex-president of the union of Swiss banks, sees the Polish situation as a *sui generis* case of insolvency. He writes, "when a people, while accepting the most extreme sacrifices, refuses to work for a government that it no longer tolerates, it becomes impossible to extract the surplus necessary to settle outstanding debts."[2] Commenting on the enormous dilemma created by the Polish debt, the French Institute for International Relations (IFRI) termed the situation "an enormous error of judgment for both borrowers and lenders." It concluded that the "problem is probably insoluble in strictly economic terms."[3]

The severity of this gigantic miscalculation might be left to the mellowing forces of time if it were unique. It was not. Unfortunately, while Poland is the worst case of East Bloc debtor insolvency, it shares its financial woes with a growing following. Romania runs a close second with an accumulated debt in 1981 of $11.5 billion to Western governments and commercial banks— $4.2 and $6 billion, respectively. Counting on its advantageous relationship with the International Monetary Fund and the World Bank to help guarantee its liquidity shortfalls, Romania looks, on the surface at least, more capable of managing its way out of an expensive credit bind. At home the problem looks grave. Basic household commodities, such as soap, are rarely available. Bread is rationed, and meat and eggs are scarce. "Luxuries" such as lemons, oranges or nuts are nonexistent much of the year. On weekends, to save costly fuel, buses no longer run except on a few main lines. And in 1982 President Nicolae Ceausescu experimented with an outrageous rationing scheme that argued that "intellectuals" would be healthier if they lived on a leaner diet than that of workers. The problem of food scarcity is more acute than during the height of World War II.

These two countries alone owe more than $40 billion, but their debt is far outdistanced by the thirst for capital in countries like Brazil and Mexico—each of which owes more than $85 billion. By 1983, Mexico's commitments totaled $90 billion and it found itself resorting to last-minute patchworks of loan arrangements and to dipping into its deflated oil reserves to meet its obligations. In a Booz Allen & Hamilton report, energy analyst Philip K. Verlerger predicted Mexicans "literally buying themselves out of financial crisis by producing oil."[4] In fact, during 1982, oil production jumped from 2.3 million barrels a day to 3 million, almost a 30 percent increase. Oil earnings, as a result of increased export sales, rose at almost twice that rate. Yet, even for this oil-rich nation, new output could only come after costly new investments in wells—and further financial credits to pay for higher production.

"What you see happening," says Gene Rotberg, treasurer of the World Bank, "is the product of human frailty. Human beings make mistakes." He describes a decisionmaking process in which immediate gratification is given priority over long-term demands. "Many financial decisions are made on the need to stay in power with no concern for the costs that are to be borne by later societies." As a result, highly unprofitable investments can be rationalized into nonproductive purposes. Of these, the thirst for ever more expensive armaments imposes a severe drain on poorer nations' foreign currency credits. By the end of the 1970s arms sales worldwide totaled almost $120 billion. Three-quarters of the heavy weapons purchases went to Third World nations. In other cases a decision might be made to finance a national airline made without any consideration for its economic viability. "The issue is not so much the debt itself but whether it is channeled into economic development uses," says Rotberg.[5]

The total cumulative debt of developing nations adds up to more than 0.5 trillion dollars. This amount is six times larger than a decade earlier. In 1981 alone the interest payments on these obligations equaled $110 billion, or an average of 20 percent of these nations' export earnings. The magnitude of the burden led the Morgan Guaranty Trust Company to write in 1980 that time had run out on the ability of Western banks to finance the deficits of the dozen most heavily indebted client nations from Brazil to Turkey.[6] Such countries as Turkey, Zaire, and Peru were felt to be on the edge of default. Signals to the banking community such as these led to a rapid drop of the rate of loans to developing nations during the first years of the 1980s.

To the borrowers, the lending institutions offered a single, clear message. Economic and social policies of debtor nations had to be revised. Stricter behavior was expected if loans were to be forthcoming. From such messages came a new service, a by-product of unlimited borrowing during the 1970s. Major financial investment houses such as Lazard Frères and Lehman Brothers Kuhn Loeb emerged as a new breed of financial management advisors to developing nations.

Such steps, much like the New York City Municipal Assistance Corporation, are not just necessary; they are vital. The problem they must correct is in many ways one of their banking peers' own doing. The lavish liberty with which credit was allowed to flow into weakening economies is a severe indictment of the professional judgment of the world banking institution. Often, more pressed by the need to outbid competing banks on fractions of points of interest, they would freely forgo careful scrutiny of credit worthiness in order to remain active players in the marketplace. Harold Lever, an ex-cabinet member and economic advisor to Prime Ministers Harold Wilson and James Callaghan, is highly critical of the performance of the world's leading commercial banks. The almost irresponsible recycling of OPEC surplus dollars into weaker countries is decried by Lever. "It would have been virtually impossible for the banks to undertake this novel, enormous and continuing recycling operation within the constraints of the domestic banking regulations of their respective countries," he states. "They had, instead, to use external subsidiaries operating in the largely unregulated Eurodollar market."[7]

WHERE MONEY IS A COMMODITY?

In the very heart of Wall Street are the trading rooms of America's leading international money-center banks. The product traded is money in the form of Eurodollars, Eurocurrencies, speculative foreign exchange purchases, domestic federal funds, certificates of deposit, or bankers' acceptances to finance international trade and government securities.

One of these money-centers is on Broad Street, where an inconspicuous entrance leads to a linoleum-floored elevator and the fifth-floor international trading room. During the morning hours the thirty to forty people gathered there are buried in a self-generated sea of shouts, hand signals, and flashing electronic messages that link them to a global network of financial brokers and data sources. In a month this trading room and nine or ten others nearby will tally a transaction volume of at least $250 billion—or an annual rate of $3 trillion dollars. This nerve center, like those of its peer institutions, is the very pulse of international finance. A torrent of orders will flow through daily, each a measure of the vulnerability of buyer and seller to seemingly inexplicable motives and movements in price.

Mason Klinck, thirty years old, a graduate of Oxford and an M.B.A. from Boston College in international finance and management, is one of the corporate traders. His visiting card says that he is an "advisor." His office, if one can call it that, is about ten square feet: a small semicircular table littered with papers, a telephone with a bank of about thirty pushbuttons linking him to his clients, mostly Fortune 500 companies, and a TV monitor flashing up-to-date figures on international financial data.

"I lifted you at 32," he shouts sharply to a colleague while one hand holds firmly onto to his phone receiver.

"That was $2 million?" comes a question in return.

To his visitor, Mason mutters: "We're so busy today, we can't keep track of all the deals we do!"

The shouting starts again with a sharp response: "That's the guy we sold $30 million to isn't it?"

"Yeah!"

"Are we square or what?"

"Canada at what? At 1.2332? OK? That was $2 million!"

A transaction has occurred. Someone just purchased Canadian dollars at a rate of 1.2332 per American dollar.

Mason has been at it for only two years here, preceded by two in other banking activities with a Swiss bank. He calls his profession a "burner." The high pace destroys. "The machismo part of this job is to come in on a Monday," he explains, "and lose. And again on Tuesday. And then try, again and again. This whole business is nerves. It takes courage, in particular when you've made a wrong decision. You have to know when to get out of a loss. The reward comes on Wednesday when you make money."

World financial news is quickly transmitted through to the trading floors such as Mason's. When AEG-Telefunken declared bankruptcy in 1982, the news reached this fifth-floor room instantaneously. The first reaction is to withhold money from this firm or any financial institution connected to it. "We quickly assume German banks are the key lenders and we are more cautious in dealing with them," says Mason. In many cases such institutions are major borrowers of Eurodollars or foreign exchange and suddenly they are themselves drawn into becoming risk liabilities by failures such as AEG's. The marketplace reacts quickly and the effect is to lead these lending institutions to raise their borrowing rates in order to lure new deposits. "It means they are short and will pay more to attract deposits to cover themselves," explained Klinck.

The Polish defaults in 1981 had even greater effects. Because of a heavy lending burden incurred by West German banks, no one wanted to risk buying Marks. The market reactions pulsed through the trading floors and demand shifted rapidly toward Eurodollars, thereby forcing their price up. Deposit rates in German banks went up accordingly.

About the short-term future, says Mason: "Further oil price reduction will resurrect fears of a worldwide shortage of dollars. This will happen mainly because producer countries will be borrowing to make up the short-fall from lost income on oil sales."[8]

In 1980, the clouded financial horizon was exposed for all to see. Within a few years, the business of international debt had a taken a new twist. Not only were commercial sources the favored credit sources over formal government loans but just the rescheduling of overdue loans accounted for almost 50 percent of the Eurocredits to Third World countries in 1981 and 1982, against one-half that in prior years.[9]

A second important twist to an untamed global appetite for capital was the business of borrowing short to finance long-term needs—emulating the experience of the corporate world. Financial capital markets, such as the Eurodollar market, provided a highly profitable device of offering short-term debt at going rates—usually high—to meet long-term debt requirements of major borrowers. The concept was not unlike a homeowner going back to the bank every six to twelve months to borrow mortgage money at the new "special rate of the week." As long as interest payments were met on schedule everything was fine; this held true until Poland defaulted in its interest payments obligations.

THE MAKING OF A "EURODOLLAR"

It is particularly ironic that one of the most freely tapped sources of capital for Western economies is an invention of Soviet and East Bloc countries. During a period of rising Cold War tensions, Eastern Bloc countries wanted to remove from American control deposits they held in the United States. These funds were placed in two Soviet-owned banks operating in Europe: the Moscow Narodny Bank in London and the Banque Commerciale pour l'Europe du Nord in Paris. The telegraphic address of this second bank—EUROBANK—led to the term "Eurocurrency."

The absence of any U.S. restrictions on the use of dollars by nonresidents rapidly attracted further deposits, as did rates of interest slightly higher than those obtainable on national markets. Several governmental actions also helped to catalyze interest in the ironic "freedom" gained from deposits in these Soviet banks and others. In 1957, British monetary restrictions were imposed to protect a weakened pound. Loans in sterling to nonresidents were restricted on one hand, and on the other, with the encouragement of the Bank of England, London financial institutions maintained their dominant position on international markets by making loans in dollars. More than anything else, however, U.S. balance-of-payments problems during the 1960s sharpened the lines of division between the domestic American market and the rest of the world. The 1963 Interest Equalization Tax helped close the New York market to foreign bond issues. Subsequent programs of the Federal Reserve would oblige American firms to finance overseas operations with money raised abroad.

OPEC's oil profits would fully mature the concept of Eurodollars as a primary device for recycling world debt. By the 1980s, even the definition of Euromarket could vary from a narrow one including only those banks operating in Europe to a wider one including Japan and offshore centers in the Caribbean. Even newer markets are now included from Singapore, Hong Kong, and Bahrain. The banking network is immense. Almost 600 banks from eighty-five nations operate outside the jurisdiction of any single nation. They control a web of 450 subsidiaries, about 5,000 foreign branches, and count approximately 1,000 affiliations—all of which are largely outside the grasp of central bank authorities.[a] The Eurocurrency market is estimated to have risen ten times in size from about $200 billion in 1972 to $2 trillion in 1982.[b]

Source: The above is paraphrased from *RAMSES 1982: The State of the World Economy,* report by the French Institute for International Relations, Ballinger Publishing Company, Cambridge, Mass., 1982, p. 129.

a. The foreign bank numbers are from *Finance & Development,* March 1983.

b. The eurocurrency estimate is from Morgan Guaranty Trust Company, *World Financial News,* October 1982.

The world market for new capital proved a vicious circle. With high-priced short-term debt used to maintain long-term capital needs, only the nations with the highest credit ratings could count on an adequate flow of new financial capital. The five leading creditor nations—the United States, Switzerland, Japan, West Germany, and Canada—suffered little, but those with the worst ratings—such as Nicaragua, El Salvador, Zaire, Uganda, and North Korea—could expect no new sources at competitive rates.

What is at risk in this overleveraged national debt picture? While Western banks' stability is clearly at stake, another more important facet to the problem has less to do with the money than it does with the politics of debt. Two opposing camps are involved.

One concerns the East Bloc nations; the other concerns the "thirsty thirteen"* developing nations.[10]

In the case of Poland's unpaid debts to a consortium of Western banks, of which a large portion of the amounts owed are due to U.S. banks, the political utility of the debt is argued by Secretary of Defense Caspar Weinberger and conservative spokesmen such as Senator Jesse Helms of North Carolina. They see a default on payments as a vital negotiating tool in U.S. relations with the Soviet Union. Another hard-line advocate of using the debt as political collateral is Felix Rohatyn. "We should recognize that the availability of large-scale credit facilities is a strategic weapon," he says. In his view it is the Soviet Union that "should be required to refinance not only Poland but all the satellite countries. The benefits of conquest should carry the burdens of support."[11] The hidden price in the implementation of such a tactical stance would require central bank assumption of losses incurred by creditor commercial banks—an expensive risk for the taxpayer to assume. Yet, in an age of $1.6 trillion defense budgets, such a policy weapon might prove more cost effective as a bargaining tool than military hardware.

The other political consideration, which applies to the thirsty thirteen, is of a very different character. Drastic austerity measures associated with any effort to meet spiraling interest and principal payments on foreign debt could indeed undermine regimes. Countries like Turkey, Zaire, Peru, or even Mexico face intensified domestic stress as unemployment rises and social demands increase. Pressure to export more and more of the domestic production base in order to meet debt payments can only be met at the expense of the domestic consumer. It does not take long for high ratios of export income devoted to debt payment to translate into a diminished standard of living. Such conditions,

---

* Note: The thirsty thirteen debtors collectively accounted for 59.6 percent of the outstanding world debt in 1980. This was accounted for as follows: Brazil 12.1%, Mexico 9.2%, South Korea 4.6%, Spain 3.9%, Algeria 3.9%, Indonesia 3.7%, India 3.7%, Yugoslavia 3.3%, Turkey 3.3%, Argentina 3.1%, Venezuela 2.9%, Egypt 2.9%, Israel 2.9%. Source: *The Economist*, March 20-26, 1982.

made worse by a recessionary decline in demand for Third World country exports and by the rapid rise in interest rates, provide an ideal breeding ground for political unrest and for the legitimizing of opposition movements—whether rightist or leftist. Willy Brandt, ex-chancellor of West Germany and the chairman of the Independent Commission on International Development Issues (known as the Brandt Commission), states the case bluntly: "As the stalemate deepens [between North and South], the danger of political instability and upheaval grows proportionately."[12]

Austerity measures do not succeed without pain for both lender and debtor nations. One out of twelve U.S. jobs are export dependent. Of these, 30 percent are sales to less developed nations. In September 1982 Joao Baptista Figueiredo, the president of Brazil, in a speech before the United Nations General Assembly, voiced a "growing feeling among many third-world nations and industrial nations that the potential of economic collapse may be the single greatest threat to world peace."[13]

One measure of such belt tightening by debtor nations is the relationship between debt payments due in a given year and the total value of goods and services exported in the same period. In some cases—Argentina, Mexico, Ecuador, Brazil, and Chile—the annual amounts due to lenders exceed the total value of exports. In Argentina and Brazil, the interest payments alone absorb almost one-half the annual value of exports. The recession-induced decline in purchases of U.S. goods and services by Mexico added up to $7.5 billion during 1982. The effect would be felt in an aggravation of U.S. unemployment rates and a new rationalization of foreign debt support by the Reagan administration, despite strong statements to the contrary during his first years of office.

For oil-poor countries, the prospects of a long, slow climb out of their burdensome debts are dismaying. With commercial lending restrained and economic growth forced into low gear, the only apparent solution is in the lending largess of world institutions such as the IMF. This pessimism is echoed in many of the world's primary international organizations—Organization for Economic Cooperation and Development (OECD), General Agreement on

Tariffs and Trade (GATT), the IMF, and the World Bank. The OECD, says the French Institute for International Relations, gives the "impression that it was gradually giving up its role as a coordinator of economic policy to become merely a source of international statistics." These institutions do not, says the Institute, "use their freedom of maneuver for the purpose of original thought."[14]

Albert Bressand, the outspoken director of the institute's annual report, *The State of the World Economy,* crystallized the meaning of the new order laid bare by the business of debt in an article for the Spring 1983 issue of *Foreign Affairs:* "The time has come to realize that the international economy can no longer be defined as, and limited to, the intersection of national economies. Rather, it is now the national economies which must be looked upon as the extension of a global and integrated system with a logic of its own. To make the point clear, let me call the global system the 'worldeconomy.'" The spiral of indebtedness brought with it a new realization. Never again could the finances of a single nation be divorced from the web of global financial relationships. One would feed on the other.

It was now evident that the institutional lending trough needs repair and that the responsibility falls to all nations. Without a formal juridical forum to mediate defaulter settlements or second-chance provisions to guide a rearrangement of loan obligations, the process of creating new order out of a chaotic burden of debt will test the statesmanship and imagination of world leaders.

If the financiers helped to keep the world afloat by redistributing billions of OPEC dollars, they also contributed to the creation of an unmonitored indebtness that many nations are now hard put to honor. Many of these nations, much like giant corporate bankrupts, must now confront the question of repayment. Could anything be learned from the corporate experience in settling debt through bankruptcy? Is there a new breed of bankruptcy managers who do indeed have solutions that might be put to work preventing future corporate collapses and settling the immense dilemma of Third World debt? In the second part of this book, the business of bankruptcy is discussed first through the more speculative and conventional side of finding profit in bankruptcy. This is followed by a look into several important new aspects of the management of corporate and national indebtedness. Whether some of the techniques applied by these new managers offer solutions to the problem of Third World debt is explored in Part III.

PART TWO

New Managers

Chapter 6
THE BUSINESS OF BANKRUPTCY

"They don't teach you about bankruptcies in business school," says one accountant. Too bad. That sort of knowledge could make you a lot of money.

Forbes, *March 15, 1982*

THE SUBJECT of bankruptcy is not only not taught in most business schools, it is assiduously avoided. At the Harvard School of Business Administration, famous for its voluminous case study files, there are only one or two major bankruptcy cases. "This is not a field which the school wants linked to its image of molding future corporate presidents," says one faculty member who did not wish to be named.

But while the discovery of profit in bankruptcy may have reached only recently into Manhattan's plushest professional offices and investment houses, it has long been viewed as a lucrative venture by a small inner group of behind-the-scenes, sometimes suspect investors. They belonged to a generation in which it was rarely considered respectable or appropriate to be associated with *bankruptcy*. Part of the negative taint associated with those looking for profit in bankruptcy was due to a long history of unethical relations among bankruptcy judges, lawyers, and trustees whose self-interest often prevailed over the legitimate claims of creditors or employees. In most cases, bankruptcy settlements focused more on the rush to divide a diminished pie than on equity or on the rebuilding of the failed corporation. For good reason, perhaps, many people looking in on these activities would label them "vulturous." All that would change in the 1970s.

Bankruptcies, small and large, became the domain of a new generation of imaginative and aggressive deal makers. The Penn Central debacle brought new respectability and unprecedented profitability to the business of bankruptcy. Eight years of legal proceedings that ensued on that case alone along with $100 million in legal and administrative fees, stimulated the appetite of a whole new coterie of specialists. Some of the nation's most expensive lawyers, accountants, and entrepreneurs emerged as a new breed of actors in what was discovered to be a highly profitable enterprise.

Wall Street's "Twilight Zone"[1]

With the nation's bankruptcy rate soaring to highest levels since 1933, speculating in corporate carrion has become Wall Street's newest and fastest growing vogue.... High powered lawyers and investment bankers are switching from takeovers to re-organizations. Before long retail brokerage houses will be providing research reports on bankruptcies.[2]

If you aren't in the business of bankruptcy, you probably haven't heard of Max Heine. Max is more than seventy years old. Since 1933, when he came to America to escape Hitler's Germany, he has been enamored by profits hidden in the securities of bankrupt railroads. He had disovered that quick maneuvering could allow him to purchase these securities in many cases at one-tenth their face value. Later, as these bankrupt properties were acquired by others or liquidated, the securities would be paid off at much higher rates—quite profitably to Max Heine. This tactic led to the creation of a special fund, the Mutual Shares Corp., more than thirty years ago to invest in prospective bankruptcy and liquidation candidates and later the Mutual Qualified Income Fund. The former is a $140 million fund that holds $11 million in securities of companies involved in formal bankruptcy proceedings.[3]

At any one time Heine juggles more than 150 investments, waiting for the right moment to resell the bargains he has acquired for his fund. Every year 2,000 annual reports might be studied and countless newspaper tips and rumors checked out. The crisis looming at Chrysler in 1979 suited his gambling instincts and he bought senior notes of the Chrysler Financial Corp. "Even if the worst happens," he said then, "the financial subsidiary will not be affected—at least not the senior notes."[4] He was ready, too, to cash in on the rising fortunes of the Phoenix-like Penn Central by investing 5 percent of his fund in its notes.

To broaden his field of maneuver he created the Heine Securities Corp. to counsel the fund on its investments. He is also the chairman of another creation—Herzog, Heine, Geduld, Inc.—a marketeer of the over-the-counter securities. The ill-fated Braniff International airline became a Heine target. So too the razor-edged future of International Harvester. In many cases, Max Heine and others in his "twilight" field gamble on the stocks and bonds of failed companies even after trading has been halted in the New York or American exchanges. Buying and selling, in most cases, still occurs with equal intensity in regional exchanges. One of them, the Pacific Exchange, has been informally labeled the "bankruptcy exchange" because so many issues are traded there during a firm's bankruptcy proceedings.

One expert in this unique speculative business is Jeff Schultz, who started teaching corporate finance at the University of Michigan after being suspended by the New York Stock Exchange for unauthorized trading. What most saw as a financial disaster when Itel's computer-leasing empire collapsed, he saw as a blossoming opportunity. Bonds trading at 42 cents on the dollar "will be worth anywhere from 70 cents to 80 cents when the company comes out of bankruptcy," he would forecast.[5] This kind of investment in what are commonly called "junk-bonds" requires a particular intuitive skill and stomach for risk. For Schultz, the game is "to find companies whose bonds are trading as if they had already gone under. If the company doesn't go bankrupt, you can make 35% every year," he says.[6]

In many cases, the process of going through a bankruptcy procedure can strip away layers of redundant debt, staff, and other unprofitable encumberances. To another twilight-zoner, Martin Whitman, when the newly reorganized company emerges from Chapter 11 "it's liquid, it has an honest, not over-reaching management and the price is right—it's probably selling at a real comfortable discount to book. And there's a lot of information about the company so there's no surprises."[7] For the knowing speculator the results can be enormous.

But for Max Heine, now slowed down in his work by his age, times are changing. In a fitting remark on the new professionalism affecting his profession, Heine says: "The people I know just aren't on the street anymore. They've been replaced by young people." His own hand-picked successor is Michael F. Price, whom he hired in 1975 as a twenty-three year-old college graduate from the University of Oklahoma. Price was tagged a few years later by the business press as one of the most sophisticated professionals at the game.

THE NEW GAME IN TOWN: Investing in Debt

They started to appear late in 1982. Within months they were the talk of the town in Wall Street. These were "debt options." A prospectus sent to lure investors in these new speculative opportunities described them as "(i) trading of financial futures contracts (and options thereon) and (ii) arbitraging cash markets in certain financial instruments and futures markets in the same or related financial instruments. . . ."[8] At first reading this technical jargon seems appealingly simple. In fact it is the tip of an iceberg that has "dizzying combinations of options" according to *Business Week*. The magazine quotes William M. Kidder, president of an interest rate consulting firm, as saying: "It will be like playing 3-D chess."[9]

One of the major attractions of this new "get-rich" opportunity is not just the prospect of a fortune at the end of the option rainbow but the very small capital amounts required to play the game. An option on a debt obligation such as a Treasury Bond worth $100,000 can be bought for as little as $3,500—the only amount at risk if things don't work out. Unlike an interest rate futures contract which obliges the purchaser to pay variances on any given day, the debt option cannot lose a speculator more than he has put in but will probably earn less than a futures contract if all goes well.

For the buyer the shopping choice will include short-term Treasury bills, medium-term two- to ten-year bonds, or long-term debt of longer maturity. To the amateur, *Business Week* offers important advice: "Experts warn against amateurs dabbling in them until the long-term price behavior of debt options—which are untested trading instruments—is better understood."[10]

Creative Lawyers

The company's profits are healthy. Investor confidence is reflected in a rising stock price. Its annual sales in 1982 were $500 million. But, unfortunately for this construction materials company, one of its product lines that accounts for 6 percent of its annual sales brought with it the threat of a barrage of lawsuits and an estimated liability of $2 billion—an amount double the total net worth of the firm. The product is asbestos and the company that manufactures products from it is the Manville Corporation, headquartered in an architecturally grandiose complex tucked into a pristine Colorado valley.

Asbestos, while long viewed as a miracle material, also developed the reputation as a killer substance, especially for those who mine it and work with it. In major asbestos-mining towns, like Thetford, Quebec, even a casual visitor cannot avoid the common sight or sound of long, painful, rasping coughs. For asbestos workers, lung diseases and other related illnesses proved widespread and often fatal. Growing evidence and legal momentum culminated in 16,000 lawsuits aimed at the Manville Corporation alone by a battery of lawyers from coast to coast. Hundreds of other companies were also charged with a failure to notify workers of known asbestos-related ailments.

Faced with a potential $2 billion liability and a likelihood of three times as many plaintiffs, the company followed the imaginative advice of its legal counsel and filed for bankruptcy on August 26, 1982. Unprecedented, the motive for such a filing would unleash a storm of disputes. For bankruptcy lawyer Michael Crames, retained by Manville, the attention is relished. For his profession, times could not be better. During the last few years, his fourteen-man firm, Levin, Weintraub & Crames, has worked on more than 100 corporate bankruptcies, including some of the largest—e.g., Braniff and White Motors. The firm now grosses an estimated $4.5 million in fees per year. In Crames's words, "it's been one major company after the another—and the problem companies have been getting bigger and bigger."[11] One of the motives for the advice to Manville is that bankruptcy law revisions, approved by Congress in 1978, allow a judge to pass judgment on any and all future claims against a debtor, a cheap and potentially easy out to a problem that other advisors had proposed be solved by public legislation to compensate the multitude of plaintiffs.

Lawyers for the 16,000 claimants, on the other hand, argue vociferously that Manville's lawyers are "manipulating to misuse the bankruptcy laws."[12]

Like a punting specialist brought in to score the winning points in the closing minutes of a football game, the bankruptcy specialist gets center stage in moments of crisis. In the Manville case, within two weeks of Crames's first meeting with corporate executives at the company's headquarters, the Denver firm had filed for Chapter 11 court protection in the U.S. Bankruptcy Court for the Southern District of New York. Not willing to stop there, Crames got the sitting judge, Burton R. Lifland, to accept a chain of dispensations that voided the company from many of the more ignominious procedures. Forms did not have to be reprinted stating "debtor in possession," payments to employees and their pensions programs were authorized to continue unfettered, and the complicated procedures of closing all existing bank accounts was substituted by a single court order to stop all payment on outstanding checks. For his firm's efforts on behalf of Manville over a three-month period, a $200,000 fee was paid.[13]

As for the Manville case, its complexities and broad implications for current and future claimants will unleash a field day of profitable activity for lawyers and bankruptcy specialists. More than fifty firms, with names like Blatt & Sales; Stutman, Treister & Glatt; and Murphy, Weir & Butler, represent the 16,000 plaintiffs. For the flexing of this legal muscle, the fees earned will be large. That few of these services can be termed "productive" to the economy does not seem to bother anyone.

For legal theorists in academe, the Manville case provides a ripe opportunity for intellectual speculation on the impact of the case. The issue of settling unfiled future claims is at the core. "A contingent claim is one which hasn't been proved yet, and it could conceivably cover claims which don't even exist yet," says Professor Philip G. Shuchman of Rutgers University School of Law. Indiana University School of Law's Professor Douglass G. Boshkoff replies, "I really don't understand how they're going to do that."[14] His words set the stage for a lengthy debate in the years ahead. Scholarly reputations will undoubtedly be built and lost on interpretations of the Manville case and other novel related filings likely to follow. The scholarship surrounding bankruptcy will thrive on the broadening of its intellectual boundaries.

Turnaround Entrepreneurs

The profitable eccentricity of buying bankrupt companies, big and small, has produced a growing Who's Who of names in the turnaround business. Those better known to the public include Peter Sprague, who used an inheritance to buy a small failing electronics firm in Silicon Valley called National Semiconductor. Today it is one of the nation's most important and largest semiconductor manufacturers. Also well known to the business world is Timothy Mellon, who developed a reputation as a shrewd buyer of small, unprofitable railroads. He now owns a potentially lucrative patchwork of interlinked lines in the northeast of the United States.

Many of the principal players are not only self-taught but proud of their intuitive skills. "You only learn the rules by going through [a Chapter 11]," says Robert Swartz, an accountant with several large bankruptcy cases under his belt. Pointing in his office to several books on the shelf he says: "You see these? One of them has all the old bankruptcy law in it, and the other has all the new bankruptcy law. I never look at either of them. This is a business of negotiations more than anything else."[15]

Many others are less known. Richard Gerrity is one of the new breed of self-taught Chapter 11 eccentrics. He likes to buy and revive bankrupt companies. From Albany, New York, he oversees interests throughout the Northeast. His favored business pastime is negotiating the purchase, and later the resale, of defunct properties. Cold-storage warehouses interest him very much. Many of these, built a generation or more ago, clutter urban skylines with their windowless concrete mass ten to fifteen stories high. Most, managed inefficiently and without anticipation of the costly impact of spiraling energy costs, lose money and fail. Buying them cheaply, Gerrity cleans out the management, attracts a prime tenant—such as the federal government, which is in need of storage space for surplus butter or cheese—and quickly finds himself with a cash cow large enough to pay off bank loans used to leverage the original purchase. The original building is then sold at a generous profit to investors who want a tax shelter and who retain Gerrity under a management contract to manage their property.

This vicarious career started for Gerrity with a plunge into the the world of bankruptcy for which he was little prepared. In 1974 his father, an Albany investor named Joseph Gerrity, found himself holding a purchase option on a large machine-tool factory that had defaulted on a loan to him and had gone into receivership. On his son's advice, the father purchased the company, believing that its real estate property alone would more than pay back the investment. They would soon find themselves, not in the real estate business, but deeply enmeshed in a highly specialized world of machine-tool manufacturing.

The saga started soon after the acquisition of Simmons Machine Tool by Gerrity. Charles Simmons III, a third-generation family member of the firm's founder, was installed as president in his father's place, and Richard Gerrity became a vice-president to watch over the new investment. The seventy year-old firm, which at its peak in World War II had 600 employees, was down to no more than sixty. Gross sales were at about $2.5 million and were from a few primary clients in the railroad business. For the next three years, Gerrity, busy with other projects, spent little time watching over the company's resuscitation. What he failed to notice was that Charles Simmons, with a free hand to manage the firm, gradually pushed it into a new direction. Simmons solicited large and complex one-of-a-kind orders from clients in areas as geographically disparate and distant as Korea and Mexico. This seemingly successful sales strategy soon proved a two-edged sword. Within a short time, the annual balance sheets showed that something had gone wrong. What were modest profits of about $500,000 in 1975 and minor bank debt liabilities, turned into losses of $500,000 by the end of 1978 and a bank debt that had ballooned seventeen times larger than in 1975.

Said Gerrity, "The company was taking in any large machine order that walked through the door. The largest orders were actually being produced at a loss to Simmons." With orders coming in calling for sophisticated machine-tooling skills and project budgets that left no room for error, the company's inexperience quickly began to show. "If anything, I was culpable by not taking the earnings decline as a sign of an engineer being at the helm more than a businessman," stated Gerrity. "He had completely turned us away from what we should have been doing, which was assembly-line work on multiple orders of the same kind of machine." One reason was an antiquated use of accounting methods. If an order of $1 million came in, there was no means of knowing whether cost overruns were being incurred as the shop-floor work progressed. Only when the budget had run out and orders sat unfinished in the cavernous shop did the books show the overrun.

By June 1978, a moment of truth approached for Richard Gerrity. A $1.2 million mortgage was coming due and banks would not extend credit beyond the $1 million already reached. "The Simmons' offered to buy me out," says Richard, "on the gamble probably that I didn't know a thing about the business and they could get the firm at its highly deflated liquidation value."

Instead, Gerrity decided to hold on and plunge himself into the unfamiliar business of turning an insolvent operation around. On a bright, warm Tuesday morning in August 1978, he called a 10:00 a.m. meeting with Charles Simmons to ask for his resignation. Confronted, Simmons argued that he had an obligation and duty to protect his customers by staying on. He refused the suggestion. Gerrity fired him and with that act terminated both a business and a social relationship of long standing between two old and distinguished local families. By noon, the board approved the firing.

In the ensuing months, after a vain and expensive attempt to sell the firm profitably to potential German buyers, Gerrity settled in for a long battle to restore stability to his firm. Crises were frequent. In January 1979, out of cash, the firm was unable to meet its payroll. Bankers refused to extend any further credit even under the threat of having the company turned over to them encrusted in their debt. In a scramble to stay alive, the company

83

sold a large machine tool off the shop floor in order to meet two weeks of payroll obligations. Then, quite unexpectedly, an order for specialized work on another firm's excess volume saved the day. Henceforth, sales of large one-of-a-kind orders were abandoned and a reemphasis on multiple orders of railroad machine tools was imposed. By year-end, a profit of $200,000 was earned and the numbers of employees rose to eighty-three.

Orders, hardly stable in a recessionary economy the impact of which fell hardest on the railroad industry, would sway the company from profit to loss month by month in subsequent years. But in another stroke of fortune in 1982, the change in location of the firm's only domestic U.S. competitor stimulated new orders for Simmons. Corporate debt is now tightly managed. A new product line of computer controlled machine tools was brought into the market-place by Tom Smith, an engineer-manager hired by Gerrity late in 1979. The horizon seems clear and profitable enough, for awhile, to allow Gerrity the flexibility of chasing after his new pastime: failing cold-storage warehouses.

Success in playing the bankruptcy game comes from knowing its unique rules. Timing is crucial. A knowing speculator has to select the right moment to buy—that critical low point between owners of bonds and securities selling out and speculators seeing an opportunity. Understanding that a court settlement can favor different classes of creditors or take many years to settle—added risks to the holders of the best-secured senior credits—is also essential. In the notorious national cases such as Equity Funding and King Resources, shareholders were given higher status than normal because their plight was seen as a result of fraudulent management activities. In many situations, though, for those speculating on the futures of companies like W. T. Grant's, the investments were lost in the final liquidation of these firms. For others who are waiting for the future prospects of touch-and-go companies like Chrysler, the rainbow is beginning to shine. Chrysler, which sold in the 50s in 1980 and down to 14 thirty months later, was back up to 27 by mid-1983.

Investors are not complaining about the metamorphosis of several other corporate disasters. Toys 'R' Us is one that spun off from a larger entity, Interstate Stores; Orion Capital Corp. was reborn from the more notorious Equity Funding Corp. of America; King Resources Co. failed in 1971 and reappeared seven years later with an appropriate new identity as Phoenix Resources Co. Such successes reap large rewards for those with the skill and intuition to buy at the right moment. Interstate stock, for example, sold at a "fire sale" price of $1/8 in 1974; when the company was reorganized and Toys 'R' Us emerged in 1978, the share value quickly jumped to $6 1/2. It now trades for in excess of $40 a share. Interstate bonds jumped nearly 9,000 percent in value.

The profitability of bankruptcy is now so attractive that special departments devote full attention to it in investment firms, law and accounting offices, and banks. A domain once monopolized by "ten cents on the dollar" barterers and manipulators now belongs to a far more respectable and professionally astute generation of business leaders. These are the new managers whose skills may prove crucial in turning the legacies of an indebted decade to constructive advantage.

Chapter 7

THE NEW
MANAGERS

There are records of insolvency proceedings in the tablets of Hammurabi in 1,750 B.C. I doubt if there is anything fundamental that is new about the subject.

Victor Palmieri

THE RELATIONSHIP between debt and bankruptcy is all too old a story. An overextension of the former through bad management, poor judgment, fraud, or merely the impact of deleterious external events frequently leads to the latter. For a corporation, accumulation of debt may involve a wide assortment of creditors from lending banks, suppliers, customers who have prepaid for goods or services, investors with money at risk, or employees whose pension funds or accumulated benefits might be at stake. In the case of a national debtor, the burdens of default fall into the laps of commercial and investment banks as well as to central banks of other lender countries. Should international defaults actually occur, the price is ultimately paid by the taxpayer whose central banks would absorb not only their losses but, in all probability, the losses of its commercial banks.

In the following pages the "new manager" is characterized by four kinds of professionals whose experiences have opened new ground in the business of bankruptcy. The first, exemplified by Victor Palmieri, is the crisis manager invited by a corporate board to remold a failing operation. An academic, Professor Edward I. Altman, whose applied research has provided the business and investment community with new bankruptcy forecasting tools, is the second. The third is a corporate lawyer, Scott Kruse, whose work is leading to a new appreciation of the labor union and employee as central figures in bankruptcy proceedings. And fourth, the new manager is characterized by the more opaque manipulations particular to the world of international banking. A rare insight by the reporters of *Euromoney* magazine into the day-to-day management of loans to national clients comes from their detailed report of a Costa Rican debt rescheduling in 1981 and 1982. The rescheduling is managed by an influencial consortium of investment and debt counselors, known in financial circles as the "troika."

1. Crisis Manager: Palmieri

In the normal course of a corporation's economic life, the dangerous flirtation between debt and bankruptcy constantly nags. Yet, even for those crossing over the brink into the protection of bankruptcy court proceedings, statistics suggest that in the case of publicly held corporations, a significant number reemerge with battle scars and losses but the wherewithal to be back in the economic mainstream.

One method of putting healthy assets of a troubled firm back to work is to invite in crisis managers to pilot the firm through stormy and unpredictable waters. In this field, few individuals in America have accumulated as much experience and favorable publicity turning around hopeless corporate operations as has Victor H. Palmieri.

Turnaround stories of demise to new stardom are Wall Street favorites. The most stunning of all was the transformation of the Penn Central Co.—the owner of the Penn Central Transportation Co.—into a thriving business still linked by name but hardly by activity. In 1978, after eight years of bankruptcy proceedings, the Penn Central Corp., stripped of its railroad operations by the federal government, resurfaced from the complex untwining of its predecessor as a diversified conglomerate operation in energy, entertainment, and real estate. It controlled some of Manhattan's plushest properties. A new entrepreneurial vision was brought to it by Palmieri, whose firm was retained to help reorganize the

Penn Central's nonrail subsidiaries and real estate assets. His firm's compensation included its direct costs, together with a share of the increases in value of the non-rail subsidiaries over a five-year period plus one percent of the proceeds of sales of the real estate assets—a cumulative compensation estimated in excess of $20 million.

Within a short time, Palmieri, who had earlier headed up the Great Southwest Corporation, which had been a subsidiary of Penn Central, would manage the sale of 13,000 parcels of land and 50,000 rental accounts including highly valued property around Penn Central Station in Manhattan. Looking back on this achievement, *Fortune* magazine labeled him "the Amazing Rent-a-Boss" in a flattering, congratulatory article. His efforts had raised nearly $1 billion in cash and turned a creditor-bound dying corporation into a healthy business enterprise. Palmieri's methods were instrumental in helping to pay off $2 billion in secured debt to an array of creditors including life insurance companies, sixty banks, and the trustee of the New York, New Haven and Hartford Railroad, whose original owners have never been fully paid since their railroad was acquired by the Penn Central. The agreed payment plan required that 10 percent of debt be paid in cash and the rest in bonds, preferred and common stock of the new entity. These stocks, issued in 1978, are now (1983) worth ten times more for preferred, and two to three times as much for common. No one is complaining.

At age fifty-three, Palmieri is not about to jump to just any new project. He doesn't need more publicity; he is already a legend in business and government circles. He doesn't need more money. With fees measured in millions of dollars per project, there is little he doesn't seem able to achieve. His firm, Victor Palmieri and Company, with spacious offices in Los Angeles and Washington, D.C., is managed by his long-time associate, John A. Koskinen, who is both president and chief executive officer.

If it is another corporate crisis he works on, it would have to be as challenging as Penn Central. The one he chose in mid-1983 was the giant insurance conglomerate Baldwin-United, with $9.3 billion in assets, most of them from invested insurance premiums.

With the sale of such assets blocked by insurance regulators, the conglomerate is faced with an excess of $600 million of short-term debts it cannot pay. To help repair this company's finances, Palmieri's firm will receive fees of $1.5 to $2 million a year and options to buy 5 percent of Baldwin's outstanding shares.

Reflecting on the troubled economic environment of the early 1980s, Palmieri is far from sanguine. "The last fifteen years," he says, "have been terrific ones during which to borrow. The problem now in a deflationary economy is paying off with expensive money. In 1982, 64 percent of corporate profits was already going for debt service. You start separating myth from reality when you look at the infrastructure. We are more of a basket case today when you consider the enormousness of the deferred maintenance."[1]

His colleague, John Koskinen, is equally pessimistic. "The worst is ahead of us," he argues, "especially if one looks at the phenomenal erosion in the quality of corporate balance sheets. How very fragile the whole system is becomes evident when we see the link between domestic and international lending. There are a lot of corporations and banks strung out waiting for things to get better."

"Quite obviously," says Koskinen, "a go-go attitude by many banks has been a vital part of the problem. It's a great irony that First Chicago, *the* aggressive lender of the early seventies, turned to a new chief executive to cut back on its overextended loans. This was at the same time that Continental Illinois was being complimented by *Fortune* and others in the late seventies as the star Chicago bank. But, today it's First Chicago that looks good."[2]

Such shifting tides of fame and grief are expected to occur with increasing speed in the years ahead. In Chapter 3, Professor Edward I. Altman was quoted as saying that 10 percent of the nation's top 2,000 corporations show signs of financial distress. Of these he estimates that one-half are what he terms "bona fide bankruptcy candidates."

A problem of such magnitude—in particular because it involves the added responsibility of protecting the interests of millions of employees, creditors, and investors—begs for resolution. To many specialists who understand the corporate culture, the likelihood of a solution coming from within is far less likely than one being induced from without. Thus arises Victor Palmieri's admonition that the only solution is to send in the "crisis management team." Sanford C. Sigoloff, a man of versatilities similar to Palmieri's and currently the CEO of The Wickes Cos., which is faced by 15,000 creditors and a $1.6 billion Chapter 11 reorganization, is a practitioner of this approach, as are many other turnaround experts whose skills and personalities are uniquely suited to crisis management. An ability to function in a pressure cooker business environment, to maintain an upper hand in the myriad negotiations essential to a turnaround, and to understand the regulatory constraints are traits commonly associated with such individuals.

Boards, in particular, tend to reject early warning signals. "They like to hear the best," says Palmieri, "and seldom do they insist on an atmosphere that would surface crisis signals." And if this is a survival reflex of American corporate culture, it is aggravated, he believes, by current bankruptcy laws as revised in 1978. Giving greater leeway to existing management to tunnel itself out of its self-made problems is not a solution. Koskinen characterizes the problem by asking: "What happens when the guys who brought you Vietnam stay on? In corporate America you get International Harvester." Adds Palmieri, "IH simply institutionalized the art of selling below cost." The price paid by such a managerial ethos was the relinquishment of control to the company's lenders, its banks. Whether their interests—which are to protect their loans—coincide with IH's needs for a long-term, capital-costly turnaround is far from evident.

In Palmieri's view, the corporate culture tends to treat bankruptcy as a management problem and not as a failing of the ingrained corporate system itself. "You must remember that this becomes a very emotional thing, especially if you are the one who has shepherded the company into dangerous waters. When the crisis hits, both from within the company and from without, the attention tends to focus on the CEO and rarely at the management system. Few corporations can take that last turn."

Given an innate resistance by an entrenched managerial hierarchy to corporate surgery, the crisis management team is a reasonable option for a board of directors to consider. The alternative, akin to putting a bandaid on a deep wound, is to bring in a new CEO and shuffle the upper management echelons in a game of musical chairs. This approach fails in two important ways. The first is that a turnaround may require only a temporary but radical infusion of survival tactics; the second is that the talents of a new CEO can be quickly neutralized by a cadre of politically entrenched managers below him.

The solution in many cases is the crisis manager team, an outside group whose efforts are aimed at a short-term restructuring of the troubled entity. Implicit in such a remedy is an understanding that unique skills not normally available to the CEO or his staff are needed for a very brief period, after which traditional management talents can again function efficiently. Not only must the new manager know how to exert full control over corporate cash and to apply quick judgment in peeling away limp assets, but the manager needs to bring into play a fresh understanding of the legal and other guidelines affecting a Chapter 11 turnaround. A corporation in financial distress is confronted, in many cases, by the unique peculiarities of two new intersecting paths—those of accounting conventions and those of federal securities laws. These are the central concerns of a professional turnaround team. As Palmieri argues, these are exactly the areas in which even the most versatile and successful CEO is probably the least well versed. Such specialized talents as those involved in negotiating financial releases, fielding stockholder suits, and establishing relations with the Securities and Exchange Commission are competences that the turnaround team brings with it.

"You have a whole new set of vectors coming into play," says Palmieri. "Most of these require a very particular mindset and an inventory of essentials that are not taught in 'B' schools [NYU is one exception]. Much of this is channeled into crisis negotiations, dealing with lawyers, partners, regulatory agencies, and people who understand capital and currency markets. When I look back at my experiences with Penn Central, it still astounds me to recall that the prevailing corporate attitude was 'why bother even trying.'"

"In such a high-risk period," adds Koskinen, "You need the right people. Not people adept at running a company over the long haul, but those fine tuned to function as a team in a crisis environment."

This philosophy became the stock in trade of Victor Palmieri and Company since his call to repair the Penn Central's post-bankruptcy nonrail properties in 1970. Working on a five-year contract, he turned the ailing operation into a solvency that few on Wall Street could have envisioned. During this momentous turnaround, his firm was appointed by a bankruptcy court to be the trustee and manager of Levitt & Sons. Owned by I.T.T. and deeply enmeshed in its quicksand of debt, it was ordered to be set loose in a ruling affected by other I.T.T. acquisitions. With a five-year mandate to mend its balance sheet and sell it, Palmieri would not only turn a year-end loss of $73 million dollars in 1974 to a profit of $4.4 million within thirty-six months, but he would also find a buyer.

This success drew in an even tougher client, the Teamster's Central States, Southwest and Southeast Pension Fund. Mismanaged and entangled in accusations and legal suits, the fund had gained further notoriety for its numerous ventures into mob-controlled real estate. Palmieri's assignment by government order was to oversee the restructuring of about $600 million of pension fund assets.

These and subsequent ventures required the consumate skills of the crisis manager working in the unique pressure cooker of financial deadlines, government orders, and court jurisdictions. "All these represent a new set of complexities even though the problem itself is old. It's an area which few corporate executives understand thoroughly. You know, if we had been at Chrysler we could have blocked for Iacocca and made his job quite a bit easier to manage. That's a case I would have bet would not have made it. He's my hero now and he appears to be making it. But. . . ."

Palmieri reflects, "I wonder how much time and energy was drained that could have been saved."

2. Academic: Altman

His office is deep in the canyons of Wall Street, but it has none of the trappings commonly attributed to those who wheel and deal in the world of finance. Professor Edward I. Altman teaches and works at New York University, where he chairs the Graduate School of Business Administration. A linoleum-covered corridor leads to a diminutive office. A coffee machine sits outside his door near his secretary. Inside his office, file boxes and neat stacks of reports, papers, and articles decorate most of the small room. Old maps of Manhattan Island and a few photographs of sabbatical ventures offer a few clues to the professor's personal interests. As he talks, he reminds his visitor of a less visible asset essential to his work: a committed student-researcher team that spends countless hours tracking what he describes as "staggering numbers of recent bankruptcies."

Eighteen years have gone by since he chose as a graduate student to focus on a field ignored by most: bankruptcy. This interest soon developed into a dissertation that combined accounting, finance, and statistics into the creation of a predictive model for corporate failures. Two years later, in 1967, Altman had created at UCLA the basis for what would become his "Z-Score Model" for predicting corporate performance. Ahead of his time, Altman subsequently developed several more refinements that acquired similar labels—the Zeta® in 1977 and A Score in 1980. These models eventually found wide acceptance and proved highly effective in allowing corporate executives, investors, and creditors to predict the effects of excessive debt; early on, in his view, the main problem was that not enough executives understood the impact excessive debt could have in destroying a corporation—in part an explanation of why corporate indebtedness rose so fast during the 1970s.

The key features of the Z-Score Model developed by Altman are disarmingly simple. Five ratios are created and combined into a weighted end-number he labeled the "Z value" or what might also be called a credit score [See chapter notes for a full description of the formula]. A firm scoring above 2.99 is in relatively sound financial health; between 2.99 and 1.81 it calls for concern and possibly remedial actions; below 1.81 it is in financial distress and has a financial profile similar to post-bankrupts. On May 17, 1982, *Business Week* published a listing of negative ratings based on a more sophisticated Zeta® model prepared by Altman and Haldeman in 1977. These showed Braniff airline scoring a prophetic -4.32 in September 1981; other airlines, such as Pan Am and Continental, had scores between -1.74 and -3.05. At the start of 1982, International Harvester rated -0.76; A&P, a few months earlier, rated -3.35. Once applied, the formulas developed by Altman often peeled away glossy veneers from apparently healthy balance sheets with high reported profits to reveal a far less healthy inner core.

To demonstrate their forecasting utility, Altman and his colleagues completed three different sets of comparisons between 1970 and 1982. They compared what is labeled by accountants as the "going-concern" judgment—meaning that a corporation is essentially sound—with the bankruptcy ratings developed by Altman. One hundred and nine bankrupt firms were compared. In three-quarters of the cases the Z-Score predicted bankruptcy two years prior to actual bankruptcy; auditor opinions were found to be accurate only one-fifth of the time. A year before bankruptcy filing, the model was more than 85 percent accurate; auditors managed a 48 percent accuracy.[3] With the Z-Score as a tool, Altman's decade and a half of corporate analyses brought him to a sobering conclusion. "Firms have become more risky," he reveals in a new book entitled *Corporate Financial Distress*. "Their average return on investment has shrunk, and the stock market's assessment of the value of equity relative to increased debt has also deteriorated."

One example, studied by Altman and actually experienced by a perceptive CEO of GTI Corporation, James LaFleur, demonstrated the fallacy of targeting and rewarding corporate behavior solely on rising profits and earnings per share. GTI, an electronics component supplier based in Pittsburgh, had spent the early part of the 1960s caught in a rush of growth fever. In Altman and LaFleur's words:

> Managers focused almost entirely on their P&L statements. They were willing to borrow what was necessary to increase sales and profits. With stock values rising, they expected to obtain very favorable equity funding in the future to pay off the accumulated debt. That strategy served well until economic downturns in 1969 and 1972. With profits falling, many companies had trouble servicing debt that had looked so easy to handle a few years earlier. But GTI, like others, refused to alter its strategic course.[4]

By 1975 GTI was losing money faster than it could make it. A year-end audit showed a loss of $2.6 million on sales of $12 million! Its Z value was 0.4, far below the critical edge of 1.81.

Using the five ratios as a guide, LaFleur, a board member turned president, looked at the five numerators—working capital, retained earnings, earnings before interest and taxes, market value of equity, and sales—to decide that immediate surgery could be applied by selling off assets—the common denominator to four of the ratios—that were not earning money. The revenues would help retire outstanding debt. That step alone pushed the Z value to a much safer 2.95. Continuous use of the five ratios as a guide ultimately helped GTI executives restore operating vigor to the firm and raise the Z value to 7 by 1979. The firm's experiences gave a more dynamic meaning to the Z-Score model by using them less as a predictive tool than as a device for charting turnaround tactics.

The importance of Altman's work is that it provides the manager with a working tool to predict and then possibly remedy corporate financial and operational problems; of equal importance, it introduces an important new external measure of company performance. The utility of this measure can prove highly beneficial to investors, brokers, loan institutions, the Securities and Exchange Commission, and others concerned about monitoring corporate activities. Most often, the outside analyst is dependent on the printed financial statement and on the auditor's judgment that the data supplied are accurate. This information rarely satisfies a need for a predictive measure of a company's future performance. The Z-Score filled this gap.

3. Crisis Mediator: Kruse

Talmadge Ellisor of Newberry, South Carolina, who was introduced in the preface to this book, lost his job because of a bankruptcy. Employed by the same textile mill for most of his productive life, he, like 370 others employed at Newberry Mills, was given a curt two-weeks' notice prior to his dismissal. He left the company without vacation pay, accrued benefits, or a pension plan. For many like Talmadge, already in their late fifties or early sixties, the loss of employment was traumatic. Not only was their dignity and economic security shattered, but the prospects of retraining or reemployment were close to nil.

The issue of employee rights in bankruptcy cases has long been overlooked to the detriment of hundreds of thousands of workers affected by bankruptcy proceedings. In some cases, like that of the Newberry Mills, the laxity of state laws themselves would be partially at fault for not legislating a corporate responsibility to establish pension fund protection for laid-off workers. In many cases, even where unemployment or pension funds are provided for, the terrain of bankruptcy offers hazy guidelines on how employees' interests in these funds might be protected.

The law and procedures for dealing with employee and employer issues under the umbrella of bankruptcy protection is new. One person helping to chart this field is lawyer Scott Kruse. While the spectacular view from his downtown Los Angeles office may at times vanish in a brown smoggy haze, Scott's professional life has all the trappings of success—an education at Princeton University followed by Harvard Law School, plush offices in the new office tower where his firm, Gibson, Dunn & Crutcher, is located. As a member of a large legal team involved in the unfolding reorganization saga of the Wickes Cos. in San Diego, as a participant in many other debtor firms' bankruptcy proceedings, and as a one-time federal mediator in labor union disputes, Kruse has accumulated a thorough grasp of the issues involved in negotiations and decisions regarding the positions of labor unions, employees, and employers during a bankruptcy proceeding. What follows are his observations.

Employer, Union, and Employee
by Scott Kruse

One constant in business bankruptcies is that employees are always affected. And in most cases, while one finds that bankruptcy is considered more and more acceptable or even routine in the U.S. corporate world, concern for the employee has yet to catch up. As a result, employer and employee relations are an increasingly contentious focus of bankruptcy negotiations. A number of options exist for dealing with these situations. One element, of particular importance as a rapidly evolving aspect of bankruptcy law and negotiations, is the role of the union (and implicitly of the non-union employee) in a Chapter 11 reorganization.

Several general goals and interests of the debtor company, its employees, the union, the multiemployer employee benefit funds, and the non-labor-related creditors in a bankruptcy or potential bankruptcy must be mediated. It is in the interaction of these that one finds the need for better cooperation and a clearer set of governing rules.[5]

In general, employee concerns are fairly straightforward. They want to be paid outstanding wages and benefits owed to them, or to maintain their wages and benefits for as long as possible, or, at best, to keep their jobs. In practice, the real choice is more likely to be between maintaining their jobs at existing wage rates or maintaining the maximum number of jobs at a lower overall wage level. Oftentimes, costly work rules and other restrictive working conditions are also put at risk.

Normally, one might assume that union objectives tend to reflect those of its employee members. In fact, union interests show a surprising divergence from those of employees. In many cases, the union may not be willing to help save jobs or even the company itself for its members, especially if the union has to share concessions with other employees. The bankrupt's employees may not share this union concern. The union's most obvious goal is to maintain the number of *union* jobs (and union duespayers) in the area or industry, as opposed to the overall number of union and nonunion jobs. When faced with the possibility of closing a plant or a purchase of the indebted company by a nonunion buyer, some unions admit privately to a preference for closure and have acted accordingly.

Another contentious subject involves multiemployer employee benefit trust funds. These are funds supported by several employers to provide for pension, health, life insurance, and other benefits. Because they serve the interests of a group of firms, trustees of these funds can diverge from positions held by the affected employees from a single bankrupt member company. The funds want to collect any unpaid contributions owed them by a bankrupt participating firm. But they also want, on one hand, to preserve jobs as the basis for future contributions and, on the other, to avoid employer withdrawal liabilities explained below. These two objectives are not always compatible.

The potential for conflict is ample, particularly in a bankruptcy case. For example, if the debtor company owes money to an employee benefit fund, trustees from competitor companies might not mind pushing for collection even if it means the demise of the debtor. Occasionally, because of a competitor's presence on the fund, a debtor firm may be reluctant to provide the fund with confidential financial information that it would be entitled to as a creditor.

Many are so underfunded that they are in no position to pay all the retirement benefits due in the future. Recently, though, new laws were passed requiring employers to meet their proportionate share of any unfunded (or underfunded) liability. This is called "withdrawal liability" because it becomes payable by the employer upon a 70 percent or greater reduction in contributions by the employer to the multiemployer pension plan. Bankruptcy proceedings frequently trigger such withdrawal liabilities because facilities are closed or sold, or because of major layoffs and liquidations.

Withdrawal liabilities can amount to many millions of dollars and can be a major factor in bankruptcies and potential bankruptcies. Moreover, these withdrawal liabilities generally do not even appear on the debtor's financial sheets, for they are only a potential liability. In or out of bankruptcy, they can significantly affect plans to close or sell portions of the business. Recent bankruptcy court decisions have held that such withdrawal liabilities are pre-petition claims that have no priority for payment, but instead must stand in line for payment with other unsecured claims. Multiemployer pension funds may have to wait for possible, partial payment later or settle for less than full payment presently. This gives employers some leverage in dealing with such withdrawal liabilities once a petition is filed or by threatening to file a bankruptcy petition.

Mediating and managing these competing interests is the task of the debtor firm. In dealing with employee interests, outside of the basic matter of keeping creditors at bay, there are useful advantages to a bankruptcy petition. Foremost is that all claims arising before the petition was filed are automatically put on hold. This temporary stay of judicial and government agency proceedings regarding all pre-petition claims can be an effective lever for the debtor in dealing with government agencies and employee or union lawsuits over pre-petition conduct and claims. With court approval, favorable settlements of such claims may be possible since the claimant's alternative is to wait for a possible partial recovery years later. If the government, the union, or individual employees are not realistic in evaluating the worth of their claims in a bankruptcy, they can be forced to wait in line with other creditors to assert their claims at the end of the bankruptcy proceeding. Management can also consider the option of getting the bankruptcy court to reject union contracts if they can be shown to be burdensome to the debtor. While this does not magically erase union claims, it can create a climate to renegotiate them.

Such advantages to a debtor must be evaluated alongside the disadvantages. Aside from the impact on future credit and the cash expenses involved in bankruptcy proceedings, employee morale, productivity and retention can be severely hampered. In a bankruptcy, a company must skillfully manage its employee relations and union relations through a carefully planned employee and union communications program and a flexible and reasonable approach to employee and union problems. In some cases this may mean that the company should not take full advantage of the normal bankruptcy rules with respect to payment of employee claims. For example, efforts to run an orderly and efficient plant or facility closedown while minimizing inventory and other losses may require authority from the bankruptcy court to pay accrued severance pay to terminated employees, despite the fact that such severance claims were pre-petition claims that could legally have been left for only partial payment months or years later as part of a plan of reorganization. Of course, other creditors may object to giving preference to employee claims over their claims. Also, if the money is not available, this favored treatment of employees is not possible. To keep key employees, it may also be necessary to devise irresistable compensation packages for such individuals—known as "golden handcuffs."

A decision to file for bankruptcy is never easy. Often the most complex issues have to do with employees. Unions may be asked to accept wage cutbacks, or to loosen restrictive work rules; similar cuts may be asked of nonunion employees. Other considerations may involve laying off employees or reducing hours; consolidating facilities; selling facilities or divisions, or even the entire company; closing parts of the company; and in the extreme case, liquidating. This is the normal range of choices; there are alternatives. One of the most publicized is the Employee Stock Ownership Plan (ESOP). In such a plan the company sells all or a portion of the company to the employees. Despite a need for aggressive entrepreneurship and unique financing arrangements—conditions not always available—ESOPs are resorted to more often.

Among the alternatives, concession or giveback bargaining is certainly given priority consideration in any bankruptcy or potential bankruptcy. By the late 1970s and early 1980s, more unions were willing to grant concessions than prior to that time. One price that companies *must* pay for concessions in almost any situation, however, is equality of sacrifice by management and nonunion employees. The company cannot expect unions alone to bear the cost of bad times. This obvious principle of equity was illustrated when General Motors tried to increase its executive bonus program just after the United Auto Workers (U.A.W.) made its wage concessions in 1982. The U.A.W. and employees were furious and the increases were rescinded.

Whether dealing with concession bargaining, a partial sale of the company to another, or even closure, there is a need for some degree of cooperation among all parties—debtor, union, employees, employee benefit funds, purchasing company, and creditors. Although their interests are not always the same, cooperation is essential to maximize results for all. Thus, if the sale of a plant is obstructed by union opposition and the plant is forced to close, no one is better off. Or if a plant winddown to closure is sabotaged and poorly run because the company or creditors refuse to allow payment of severance pay or employee benefits, then the return on those assets may be less for all. Practicality is a key to success.

In some cases involving a larger company and multiple unions, debtor companies have established special labor-management committees with their unions and sometimes employee funds also to deal with the problems and communications associated with bankruptcy. From the company's perspective, such an informal labor committee may be preferable to a formal court-appointed labor creditors committee particularly if the employees, unions, or employee benefit funds are large creditors of the company. One major disadvantage to the company of a court-appointed labor creditors committee is that the debtor company will have to pay the expenses of the committee members and possibly the fees of counsel and accountants for the committee, subject to bankruptcy court approval of the expenses.

On occasion, a committee might waive its expense claim. An unpaid, informal committee, if appropriate in the circumstances of the case, can maintain contact between the company, unions, and employees on facts and developments in the course of a bankruptcy proceedings. In addition the company might use the committee to marshal union and employee support before the bankruptcy court; or to assist the company in building a case before creditor committees prior to the final plan of corporate reorganization.

All the tasks involved in pulling together the divergent interests affected by a bankruptcy are formidable. The stakes involved are high for all parties. The company needs the employees and their cooperation, and it needs the participation of their unions and employee benefit funds if it is to pull the company out of its financial difficulties. Likewise, the employees, unions, benefit funds and creditors have no choice but to cooperate if they hope to derive any advantage.

The stakes may transcend the survival of particular companies and jobs or the payment of debts owed. Indeed, the vitality of the American economy itself might be challenged—as was clearly argued in the Chrysler call for a federal loan guarantee. Properly handled, today's financial crises can become the basis for a more cooperative relationship between labor and management if both parties are willing to make the necessary effort and sacrifices.

4. Reschedulers: The "Troika"

In August 1982, *Euromoney* magazine published a very unusual article. Step by step it followed the rescheduling of $240 million owed to an array of investment and commercial banks. What is unique about the article, which is reproduced in full below, is its initimate look into the machinations that characterize the business of international lending. Emotions run high, threats are made, and conflicting interests clash. It reveals, too, the work of highly professional managers of international debt rescheduling, in this case the troika of Lehman Brothers Kuhn Loeb (New York), Maison Lazard (Paris), and S. G. Warburg (London).

The author is particularly grateful to Euromoney Publication Limited in London for the authorization to reproduce the article. It ran as follows:[6]

The story of Costa Rica's rescheduling may one day become a case study for banking schools. It is a story of conflict: not between a busted central American state and its bankers, but between its bankers. In essence, it is an insight into the different outlook and traditions of investment bankers, on the one hand, and of commercial banks on the other.

When Costa Rica was unable to repay its loans in late 1980, three groups of creditors were involved. One group consisted of holders of notes and bonds, with the issues' lead managers Banque Nationale de Paris, DG Bank and European Banking Company as prominent defenders of their rights. Another group consisted of participants of syndicated credits, organized in a 10-bank steering committee led by Bank of America. The third group was formed by seven of the 16 participants in a short-term credit that was lead managed by Libra Bank International. It was natural enough that the three groups should look after the interests of their members; otherwise there was little point in forming the groups. But some of the parties went a long way in promoting the interests of their group. To make the situation even more complicated, some participants were in more than one camp.

It quickly became apparent that a conflict was going to be engineered. The credit participants, through the steering committee, were concerned that the holders of bonds and notes would get preferential treatment. The bond lead managers did not wish to participate in any general discussion of the rights of the creditors because participation would be an admission that there was something to discuss. They preferred to rely on the special status accorded holders of bonds and notes by legal contract and tradition.

The third group of creditors didn't want to discuss or negotiate anything. It immediately began separate legal proceedings in the New York Supreme Court for the repayment of $40 million credit. That group's case was that it had priority over all other creditors because its loan should have been paid from receipts from exports of the Costa Rican sugar crop as those receipts were received. By instituting legal proceedings, the group effectively removed itself from the scene of the growing conflict.

Ironically, Costa Rica's problems do not stem from the traditional sources in many developing countries—the political and economic paralysis of a corrupt dictatorship—but from the inherent weakness of a parliamentary democracy. Instead of being able to introduce instruments of monetary and fiscal control by decree, the government had to attempt to get new legislation passed by Congress. The government party did not have an absolute majority: Congress refused to pass the legislation.

In 1976 and 1977 coffee prices boomed: Costa Rica's government reaped a rich revenue harvest from an added value tax on coffee exports. With an election due in 1978 it embarked on a massive spending programme. When coffee prices dropped, expenditure kept on rising. The budget deficit reached record levels and, with public and private consumption out of control, the overall balance of payments deficit quickly mounted.

Hernan Saenz became Minister of Finance in 1978. Even before taking office he had a stabilization plan ready. His proposals continually frustrated by Congress, Saenz resigned in May, 1981. One of the first institutions he set up was the Department of External Financing, with Raul Fernandez as the first director, to bring order to Costa Rica's external borrowing. Fernandez outlasted his mentor by a mere six months.

As the conflict between the parties unfolded, it seemed that Costa Rica would become the testing ground for the sanctity of the position of precedence that bonds are accorded over other debt. At no time did Costa Rica want or request a rescheduling of bonds or notes, and it was continuing to pay interest and principal on publicly issued securities. The steering committee took the initiative and threatened to suspend all rescheduling negotiations unless securities debt was downgraded to equal status with loans. Costa Rica did not have the power or the legal right to do that unilaterally, but offered to try. The response from the bond lead managers, led by European Banking Company, was immediate and unequivocal—stick to the terms of your issues or we will ensure that you don't get any of the money you so badly need from the supranational agencies.

European Banking Company was fresh from the Adela affair. A $25 million floating rate note issued by Adela and managed by European Banking and Baring Brothers had just achieved the distinction of becoming the first publicly listed Eurobond to be rescheduled. That rescheduling hurt the tradition that a bond is sacrosanct. The rescheduling was forced by banks in an effort to salvage something from the $240 million they were owed or managed. Had the banks not forced, and the bondholders accepted, equal treatment, the result would have been liquidation, from which there would have been nothing for anybody.

In the case of Costa Rica the bondholders would always have some assets to seize if the banks or Costa Rica tried to force rescheduling on them. Eventually, Costa Rica and its creditor banks set up a study group to investigate the situation. The report of that study group stated: "Any arrangement based on non-consensual restructuring entails the risk of suit and attachment and other action, legal or otherwise, being taken to seek satisfaction of the original contract which has been breached by the non-consensual restructuring."

Although there are obvious differences between the situation of a

105

country and a private corporation in rescheduling debt, the principle of the special position of securities is no different. In the case of Costa Rica, just as with Adela, it was the principle that was at stake. The principle could not be defended in Adela's case, but it could and would be in Costa Rica.

Bondholders traditionally have relied on three valid arguments, irrespective of whether the bonds are corporate or sovereign issues, when the precedence of their debt is questioned. The first argument, sometimes referred to as the widows and orphans argument, is the protection of small investors in securities. In Costa Rica that argument hardly applied because most of the securities were in the form of floating rate notes, and were almost entirely held by banks.

The second argument is the legal standing that is accorded to securities. Under most countries' laws, securities are traditionally accorded a higher position than most other forms of debt. That is because the issuers and managers have sought such a position and won it by meticulous legal drafting in order to protect their investors. Only banks participate in syndicated loans and prudential rules and laws protect them from the consequences of over-exposure with any one creditor. The rewards of commercial lending are high and the risk should be commensurate. Besides, it has long been recognized that legal drafting for syndicated loans is inadequate. It is the responsibility of lenders to achieve higher legal standing and protection for their credits. Before that can be achieved there has to be closer collaboration between international bankers. But, as one banker wryly commented: "While you are talking to a fellow banker about tightening up contracts he will be nodding in agreement but you know that behind that nod he is already working out ways to take advantage of you."

The third argument in favour of bondholders, particularly of sovereign issues, is that bonds back the financial reputation of a country. According to the investment bankers it was, therefore, unreasonable of the commercial banks to attempt to force Costa Rica to act dishonourably by repudiating its commitments.

From the onset the steering committee of the commercial banks sought to protect the interests of its members. To do so by attempting to bully Costa Rica into a dishonourable course of action demonstrated a lack of honour among the commercial banks, according to the investment bankers.

The following is the inside story of a debt rescheduling. It is a blow-by-blow account of approximately 20 months in the life of Costa Rica, and of its negotiations to reschedule its debts.

London, October 14, 1980. $40 million loan signed with Lloyds Bank International and Midland Bank International. Wasn't to know at the time but this was the last medium-term syndicated loan for Costa Rica. Negotiations start with the IMF for a three-year extended facility fund.

Madrid, May, 1981. Hernan Saenz, Costa Rican Minister of Finance, resigns during the Inter-American Develoment Bank meeting. Loss of best known and most credible member of the cabinet is a severe blow.

Cadogan Square, London, June 7, 1981. First meeting with major commercial bank creditors. Costa Rica invites the banks to form an advisory committee but the proposal is rejected.

It is a strange meeting. Neither side comes close to understanding the other's point of view. The Costa Ricans attempt to explain their country's position and the urgent steps they see as essential to the resolution of the problem. Medium and long-term debt has to be refinanced and short-term debt rolled over.

The commercial banks seem unable to grasp Costa Rica's urgent need for foreign currency. They ask for detailed economic data; the Costa Ricans don't have it. The Costa Ricans say they are about to appoint independent investment bank advisers, a move they hope will convince the bankers of their responsible attitude. To their surprise the commercial bankers torpedo the proposal and instead, offer to advise Costa Rica themselves.

When the Costa Ricans enter the meeting they are confident the creditor banks will understand their country's problems, as the Costa Ricans see them, and relieve its foreign currency shortage. (The earlier introduction of exchange controls and a dual exchange rate have done little to halt the flight into dollars or the flight of those dollars to Miami, the traditional last resting place of hot money from Latin America.)

The bankers, for their part, refuse to believe the country is in such a mess and want clarification. The net result is to undermine bankers' confidence in Costa Rica. What was left of its credit rating is destroyed, and a solution to the country's problems is further away than ever.

Washington, June 17, 1981. After six months of negotiations agreement is reached with the IMF, but it comes too late.

The uncertainty surrounding the IMF facility held up fresh

commercial bank credit. As Costa Rica's foreign currency shortage becomes more acute the government takes further desperate internal measures to alleviate the situation. But these measures break the terms of the IMF agreement. Costa Rica finds itself locked in a downward spiral which is gathering impetus.

New York, July 15, 1981. The troika—Lehman Brothers Kuhn Loeb, Maison Lazard and S.G. Warburg—is appointed adviser for the rescheduling of debt. The fee is $500,000 for six months' advice. It is the lowest fee tendered, and, as the troika has considerable experience of rescheduling, Costa Rica does not hesitate to engage it.

San José, July 27, 1981. A telex is sent to all creditors of Costa Rica, asking them to report all their loans. It also informs them that no repayments of principal on short-term debt will be made.

San José, August, 1981. After 10 months without receiving any foreign capital, Costa Rica suspends payments of principal and interest to commercial banks, but continues to service debt to supranational agencies, as well as bonds and FRNs.

(During 1979, Costa Rica received more than $400 million in foreign medium-term loans, with less than half coming from commercial banks. The country, therefore, cannot afford to offend the supranationals.)

The government requests aid from the US and other friendly countries, but everybody, it seems, is having problems.

White and Case appointed legal advisers.

New York, September, 1981. Libra Bank starts legal action against Banco Nacional de Costa Rica, the largest commercial bank in the country, and the recipients of a short-term facility last December.

Racquet Club, New York, September 25, 1981. Second meeting with major commercial bank creditors. A steering committee of banks is formed. Banks ask for additional economic information and *pari passu* treatment of creditors, including holders of bonds and FRNs. The main concern of the banks is the non-payment of interest.

The commercial banks appear determined to set a precedent over rescheduling bonds. Citibank, as a manager of one of Costa Rica's $20 million FRNs, has just seen the latest coupon payment to holders of the bonds, but, at the meeting, its representative says he would have preferred the payment not to have been made. The commercial banks' insistence on equal misery shocks the Costa Ricans.

It's a bad meeting. As one Costa Rican negotiator leaves the hotel he is heard to mutter:

"It is difficult to understand how a country, which was a good risk so recently, arrives in the position of being unable even to pay interest."

San José, October 30, 1981. A proposal for the reconstruction of public external debt is mailed to the steering committee banks. It says: Principal and interest on publicly issued securities is to be paid on time; short-term debt is to be rescheduled over five years, with three years grace; principal of medium and long-term commercial debt is to be rescheduled over 10 years, with five years grace; and commercial banks should provide additional capital so that Costa Rica can pay interest arrears to commercial banks. (Cosmetic capitalization of interest.)

San José, November 2, 1981. An information memorandum is sent to all creditors stating that total public sector external debt amounts to $2.7 billion, of which $1.1 billion is owed to commercial banks.

New York, November 13, 1981. Because Costa Rica continues to pay interest on bonds and FRNs, banks threaten to suspend all negotiations until Costa Rica changes this policy. The mission representing commercial banks has specific instructions to force a change in Costa Rica's policy. Under great pressure, the Costa Rican representative agrees to try to renegotiate bonds and notes in the hands of banks and similar lending institutions. Costa Rica sees it as a desperate compromise designed to placate commercial bank creditors so that the talks can continue.

The offices of S.G. Warburg, London, November 16, 1981. A meeting with lead managers of publicly issued securities (Banque Nationale de Paris, European Banking Company, DG Bank, Nomura and Banque Gutzwiller, Kurz, Bungener) is held to inform them that the commercial banks' steering committee has demanded that publicly issued securities should be treated in the same way as commercial debt. They are told the government can no longer resist commercial bank pressure and that it has agreed to refinance bonds and FRNs in the hands of banks and similar lending institutions.

109

Other institutions and persons will be paid when due. Lead managers indicate that, since they are not trustees, they cannot represent bond holders, and, therefore, cannot agree to the proposal.

New York, November 19, 1981. The meeting with the steering committee is suspended. Citibank is not happy with the Costa Rican statement regarding the refinancing of bonds. Costa Rica is still making coupon payments on its bonds. The commercial banks insist they must stop. Again, they threaten to call off the negotiations. "They insist on *pari passu* treatment, without considering that bonds are bearer notes," complains a Costa Rican negotiator as he wearily leaves the meeting.

St. Moritz Hotel, New York, December 9, 1981. Third meeting with major lenders and first formal meeting with the steering committee of bank creditors.

It is another gloomy meeting, made all the more so by being held in the basement of the hotel. In the windowless room, both sides seem further apart than ever. In spite of the economic and financial information provided, many banks still cannot believe that Costa Rica does not have the funds to pay interest. Privately, some banks question the usefulness of negotiating with a government just before an election, especially as it looks certain to lose.

The banks reject the Costa Rican proposal and present a counter proposal, defined as a temporary extension agreement. The main point of the proposal is payment of interest arrears and payment of current interest as it falls due. In the first month those payments amount to about $207 million. Because of the size of the payment the proposal cannot be accepted.

The banks do not think the new policy for bonds and notes is satisfactory. In order to have a technical framework within which to discuss the issue, the idea of having a study group is discussed. The study group would be composed of a representative of the steering committee, a Costa Rican negotiator and an expert on legal matters related to bonds.

At the banks' request, the Minister of Finance makes a statement concerning the intention of the government to pay interest arrears as soon as possible, indicating that an agreement with the IMF should be reached first. The banks are seriously concerned about the possibility of capitalization of interest arrears.

Sonesta Beach Hotel, Key Biscayne, January 14, 1982. Second meeting with the steering committee of bank creditors.

Fourth meeting between Costa Rica and major creditor banks. The Costa Rican Finance Minister's love of Miami, and dislike of New York's winter weather, explain the new venue. Instead of the gloomy subterranean room in New York, the meeting place is in the sun among swim-suited holiday makers. But the two sides are as far apart as ever.

Costa Rica agrees to study and present a proposal to implement an extension agreement. In other words, it will begin paying interest again. There are indications that, if the economy improves during 1982, some portion of increased foreign exchange earnings could be made available, but it would be unreasonable to expect that such additional money would make a significant dent in the $225 million required for an extension agreement.

The study group for bonds and notes is formed: José de la Cosa, Citibank, Raul Fernandez for Costa Rica and Keith Clark from the lawyers, Coward Chance, London.

The banks are extremely disappointed with the inability of the government to pay interest and to make substantial progress with the IMF. Exchange rate policy and the deficits of public institutions and the Government, are the main problems.

It is clear to all parties that it is going to be impossible to arrive at any agreement without additional external funds, which would have to come from supranatural institutions, bilateral aid or commercial loans. To get supranational institutional funds, agreement with the IMF is fundamental. Most of the projects of the World Bank are conditional on such an agreement. Bilateral aid is also conditional on an agreement with the IMF. In addition, it is understood that governments will wait until after the elections so that they can deal with the new authorities. Commercial loans are out of the question. Accordingly, the possibility of an agreement between Costa Rica and the banks depends on the ability of the Costa Ricans to take the necessary economic measures that will make possible a viable agreement with the IMF.

The next meeting is scheduled for mid-March. The Minister of Finance indicates that he will bring with him members of the new government to be elected in February.

Sonesta Beach Hotel, Key Biscayne, January 15, 1982. First meeting of the study group on bonds and notes. It appears that the main difference between Costa Rica's rescheduling and other restructurings is in the importance that commercial banks put on the necessity of a *pari passu* treatment of bonds and notes along with commercial debt. The pressure has been on since the meeting in

111

September. The steering committee has been insisting that they will not negotiate any sort of agreement before Costa Rica accepts the *pari passu* principle.

Costa Rica has resisted the requirements of the commercial banks for three months; it was paying principal and interest on bonds and notes until the end of November.

Costa Rica has never wanted to be the first country since the Second World War to refinance publicly issued securities. Also, it is concerned about the legal action that individual bondholders might take. In addition, the procedures to be used, and their effectiveness, are proving difficult to establish because bonds are bearer instruments. Even after the meeting in October, in which Costa Rica consented to the idea of restructuring at least a part of the securities, differences between the two sides persist.

At this meeting the Costa Ricans propose that the parties to the rescheduling, banks and similar lending institutions which hold bonds, FRNs or any other securities issued by any Costa Rican borrower, should have their bonds rescheduled. Only bonds held by natural persons are excluded from the rescheduling. By agreeing to this Costa Rican proposal, the banks are already departing from the concept of *pari passu* treatment.

The banks don't seem to notice the subtle change.

During the meeting the study group is official constituted and agreement reached on the procedures and terms of reference. They include: Consideration of the potential range of holders of bonds and FRNs; the identification of actual holders of bonds and FRNs; the methods of altering payments on bonds and FRNs under, or in accordance with restructuring requirements, and the implications of altering payments and the methods used; to recommend that bonds and FRNs should be the subject of alteration of payments under, or in accordance with, the restructuring requirements.

February 4, 1982. The European Banking Company, and specifically, its chief executive, Stanislas Yassukovich, reacts strongly to the requirements of the steering committee regarding bond restructuring. He sends a telex to the Costa Rican negotiators which shocks them. First he effectively supports their resistance to rescheduling the bonds. Then he warns of the dire consequences to Costa Rica if they give way to the pressure from commercial banks.

Whilst entirely accepting the fact that you are making every effort to resolve your present situation your telex of January 28 contains evidence of a fundamental and persistent misunderstanding. Until this fundamental misunderstanding is clarified progress towards resolving these present difficulties will be impeded.

You refer to the meeting which took place in London on November 16th between your government's representatives and the lead managers of Costa Rican issues. Whilst this meeting was of course useful, it should have been explained to you by your advisers that the lead managers of Eurobond issues do not represent the noteholders and have no right to commit noteholders to any arrangements or to negotiate on their behalf. The lead managers are not the proper medium of communication with noteholders either, since they are not in a position to ensure that all bearer noteholders are in receipt of any form of communication. In this respect the lead managers of your bond issues are not the same as the committee of creditor banks who have the right to represent all the commercial banks. This is only the beginning of a basic misunderstanding which persists about the nature of the contract your government entered into when it issued its bonds.

You refer to the requirement of your commercial bank creditors that all bonds and FRNs held by non-natural persons be included in any rescheduling. The commercial banks have no right to make such a requirement since you are not in a position to meet it. This request by the commercial banks is an entirely unreasonable one and is clearly made in ignorance of the legal and technical characteristics of your contractual obligations under the terms of the bond issues.

No distinction exists between so-called natural and non-natural persons since, as any legal adviser will explain to you, the rights of bondholders are uniform, regardless of their nature. It is most unfortunate that this misunderstanding should have arisen because it has placed your government in an invidious position. Whilst you are correctly pursuing negotiations with your commercial bank creditors utilising the legal process called for in the documentation relating to your commercial bank loans, you appear to be neglecting another important group of creditors, namely your bondholders and, what is far worse, you would appear to have been willing to entertain a repudiation of your obligations with respect to some of these bondholders without any attempt to seek their consent.

The Costa Ricans are in agreement with the points covered in Yassukovich's telex, particularly on distinguishing between the bonds held by one category of persons and those held by other categories of persons. They agree that the anonymity of the bond market should be preserved and that the proposal of restructuring is an attack on the principle of bearer securities.

However, the Costa Ricans are not happy with the threat contained in the same telex from Yassukovich.

We are very anxious to do everything possible to assist Costa Rica in resolving its difficulties as long as its negotiations with creditors proceed according to law and the code of obligations generally accepted as the basis for international financing. However, if your commercial bank creditors insist on forcing you to violate this code of obligations and if you accede to this pressure, we shall campaign vigorously to ensure that you become ineligible for any financing from the multilateral institutions.

We take this view because we believe that the integrity of the international capital market is at stake and this is a more important issue than the difficulties of any single country.

Neil Balfour, European Banking Company, will explain the problems to the members of the new government of Costa Rica after the February elections.

San José, February 8, 1982. Luis Alberto Monge, Partido Liberacion Nacional (Social Democrat), wins the presidential elections.

San José, February 10, 1982. A mission of economists from the banks' steering committee visits Costa Rica to gather information.

London, February 18, 1982. The first draft of the study group report, drafted by Keith Clark, is distributed.

At this stage, one of the most important agreements reached by the members of the study group, is that it is not necessary or appropriate to seek to differentiate between different categories of holders.

San José, March 11, 1982. Raul Fernandez suggests several changes to the study group report. One of his suggestions is that the study does not adequately demonstrate the problems, particularly the technical problems, that exist in any attempt to restructure the bonds and notes. He is also concerned about the possibilities of a non-consensual restructuring because that would certainly be contrary to the legal framework of the agreements. The study group report says:

Non-consensual restructuring of bonds would entail the debtors failing to satisfy the terms of the contract without the consent of the other party and therefore being in breach of that contract and subject to suit. Non-consensual restructuring entails the debtors seeking to make arrangements to service existing contractual obligations otherwise than in accordance with their terms but instead in accordance with imposed formulations of the debtor. Restructuring agreements themselves succeed on the basis of debtors and creditors agreeing together to vary the terms of the contract by mutual agreement. Any arrangement based on non-consensual restructuring entails the risk of suit and attachment and other action, legal or otherwise being taken to seek satisfaction of the original contract which has been breached by the non-consensual restructuring. Predicting the extent of this risk is, of course, very difficult.

New York, March 16, 1982. The steering committee of the commercial banks meets mainly to discuss the reports of the banks' economists. The meeting focuses on the fiscal deficit, the multiple exchange rate that is in force and the IMF agreement.

Venice, May 1982. General meeting of the Association of International Bond Dealers.

With Yassukovich's support, two resolutions are passed and become general recommendations by the AIBD to its members. They are:

"Where the general indebtedness of a borrower is the subject of a rescheduling, any changes in the terms and conditions governing international securities (as defined by Article 2 of the Statutes of the AIBD) can only be accomplished with the necessary degree of consent of the holders of such securities, as provided for in the terms and conditions of the said securities. Procedures followed to gain the necessary level of consent of such holders must be those laid down in the terms and conditions;" and

"No attempt should be made to cause any holders of bearer securities to identify themselves, via affidavits or other methods, as a condition of the continued servicing of such securities, or in order to permit separate negotiations with some holders, except as provided for in the terms and conditions of the said securities."

Those two resolutions anticipate the study group report, which, subsequently says:

All relevant indebtedness is due from a debtor to a creditor under the terms of the contract. The restructuring agreement will amend with the consent of both the debtor and the creditor the terms of certain indebtedness due to the creditors party to that Agreement who will probably be banks. Bonds represent legal rights of action

115

(choses in action) which (by endorsement on their reverse) incorporate the terms of the contract between the issuer and the bondholder. The servicing of the bonds can be altered consensually by three methods:

A. by a resolution of a necessary percentage or number of the holders of the relevant instruments under the terms of issue;
B. by each individual relevant holder agreeing on an alteration to the terms of his instrument; and
C. by the exchange through individual agreement of the relevant instrument for another instrument or some other satisfaction.

San José, May 8, 1982. New government takes office.

Between February and May, there have been no substantial negotiations. Banks, international organizations and the IMF are awaiting the announcement of the new cabinet members and other top officials of the Costa Rican government. Any recovery plan requires strong measures, so it would not make sense to discuss the issues of restructuring with the government leaving office.

The deterioration of relations between the parties of President Rodrigo Carazo and the President-elect, Luis Alberto Monge, prevented them working together in the three months between the elections and the new administration taking office.

London, May 21, 1982. Second draft of the study group report, incorporating the comments of the Costa Rican representative.

Helmut Stromeyer, from Bank of America in Caracas, visits Costa Rica to meet the new government and to inform it of the bank's point of view towards the rescheduling.

London, June 4, 1982. Final draft of the study group report.

The recommendations of the study group is, as expected by the troika, more liberal than the view held by the commercial banks or the steering committee, which regard *pari passu* treatment as essential.

Among other practical difficulties, the anonymity of the bondholders, and the absence of trustees in the legal documentation, result in the study group recommending a consensual restructuring.

The legal rights of bondholders are protected and it is they who decide if they want bonds to be restructured or not. It is reasonable to assume that very few bonds will be presented for rescheduling.

The study group reports that: "Consensual restructuring of bonds must be preferable to non-consensual restructuring; it is not appropriate or necessary to distinguish between different types of holders or owners of bonds in determining the extent of a bond restructuring, particularly if the restructuring is consensual; the ascertainment of the identities of different types of holders, or owners, of bonds, at any given date is, in practical terms, unlikely, especially in the case of public issues."

The study group recommends that the restructuring of bonds, should, procedurally, take place either by way of exchange offers or by way of individual agreement by persons holding bonds at the relevant time. This means that the restructuring will be done with the consent of relevant parties. The worst fears of the bond lead managers are allayed with the recommendation that:

"The exchange offer can be presented to the bondholders only when the terms and conditions of the restructuring with commercial banks has been agreed upon, otherwise it will be impossible to establish *pari passu* treatment among creditors."

It is clear that with the implementation of these recommendations there will not be *pari passu* treatment among creditors. On the other hand, banks will not be in a position to blame Costa Rica for the results since Costa Rica has been acting in good faith.

St. Moritz Hotel, New York, June 8-9, 1982. Third meeting with the steering committee of the banks, the fifth meeting between Costa Rica and the major bank creditors.

This time the negotiators have been elevated to a conference room on the top floor of the big hotel with a wonderful view of Central Park. A big improvement on the basement of the same hotel, where last December's meeting took place. The different ambience is, perhaps, in anticipation of the results of the meeting and certainly has been a change from all previous meetings.

This is an important meeting for several reasons. It is the first with the new government of Costa Rica and thus, there is more hope. Also, it is the first meeting for almost five months, during which time there was little progress in negotiations and no payments of principal or interest.

This time, banks have a better knowledge of the economic and fiscal difficulties of Costa Rica. Their understanding of Costa Rica's limitations is important in determining just how much Costa Rica can afford to pay.

The Costa Rican delegation is: Federico Vargas, Minister of Finance; Carlos Manuel Castillo, President of the Central Bank; Rodolfo Silva, special presidential adviser in charge of debt; Olivier Castro, Financial Director of the Central Bank; and Raul Fernandez, adviser (resigned as Director of Public Credit in November, 1981).

The troika is also present at the meeting. This is an unpleasant surprise for the banks. Nevertheless, the Costa Ricans make a clear statement of their intention to take the painful measures necessary for economic recovery, and to arrive at an agreement with the IMF as soon as possible. The highlight of the meeting is the presentation of an interim payment plan, which affirms that on July 15 Costa Rica will start to make interest arrears payments of $6 to $10 million each month. It is expected that after an agreement with the IMF there will be some capital inflows, so the plan should generate monthly payments of about $20 million. These payments will be shared out among all creditors, including commercial banks, and holders of bonds, FRNs, and certificates of deposit issued by the Central Bank in favour of local companies.

The plan is that: 10% of net export revenue receipts will be controlled by the national banking sytstem (export receipts of the national banking system are averaging $70 million a month); 20% of additional receipts emanating from exchange controls will be collected by the national banking system; and 30% of net, non-tied capital inflows will also be collected and committed to honour debt service payments.

The Costa Rican proposal assumes that these funds will be deposited in an account of the Bank for International Settlements. The banks, however, reject that proposal.

It is then agreed that payments are going to be made directly to each creditor for interest and capital in arrears on a pro-rata basis. The banks will meet among themselves to resolve how they want to be paid. Even though they will be receiving a small amount of money, the bankers are more than pleased with this new plan in which Costa Rica assigns some priority to debt service, and recommences payments, after almost eight months in which the commercial banks have not received any payments.

Another important outcome of the meeting is the approval, in principle, by both parties of the recommendations of the study group report. What happens if only a few bonds are exchanged is still an open question. Probably the major commercial banks will try to impose non-consensual restructuring by way of requesting that those bonds which are not exchanged should not be paid. On the other hand, for the majority of commercial banks the rescheduling of bonds is not fundamental, so they will probably not allow a suspension of the refinancing agreement for further negotiations because that would jeopardize, or, at least, further postpone their payments.

London, June 1-12, 1982. Rodolfo Silva and Raul Fernandez meet separately in London with the lead managers of the bond issues and with some of the agent banks. The purpose is to brief them on the Costa Rican economic situation and to inform them of the negotiations with commercial banks. (None of the banks that have acted as lead managers or agents of bonds or FRNs are represented in the steering committee.) Specifically, the meeting discusses the recommendations of the study group report. The report is well received, especially as it is far removed from the initial statements made by the commercial banks. It will only allow for a specific restructuring, if it is implemented.

London, June 18, 1982. A common statement is agreed between the steering committee and Costa Rica on the study group report, and this, basically, quotes the recommendations of the report. Another meeting is scheduled for the beginning of August. The date will depend on discussions with the IMF. The idea is to arrive at the new meeting with an agreement with the IMF in hand. It has been approved by the staff of the IMF, but not yet by the Board.

Even with this elaborate homework in place, another year would go by before a more comprehensive rescheduling of Costa Rica's debt would be agreed to by all parties. For its client, the troika had done its work.

In each of the cases described in this chapter, the new managers proved highly skilled in focusing analytical and negotiating energy on a single overriding goal: achieving agreement to all parties' financial advantage. Whether their unique skills provide answers to the bigger financial crisis of world debt is the subject of the next two chapters.

PART THREE

Solutions

Chapter 8

NATIONAL DEBT —WHO PAYS?

"You have an amount of debt. You don't have to repay that. The roll-over of a debt is a normal thing."

"How much longer can Brazil repay old debts with new ones?"

"Well that is what everybody does. There is a very interesting saying that 'debt was not made to be paid.' So this is the case for the individuals, for the companies, for the countries."

"So you're not thinking of repaying anytime this debt?"

"Oh no! I think a country has not to be thinking of that in terms of international banking community."

Comments by Ernane Galveas, *Brazil's Minister of Finance, in answer to questions during a U.S. television broadcast in 1983*

WHETHER MR. Galveas meant to suggest that repayment of the debt was less important than constant renegotiation of continued obligations is not totally clear. Part of the clarity may have been lost in his use of English. What is evident, however, is that Brazilian authorities have built an immense edifice of foreign obligations—so immense that the likelihood of repayment to lenders such as New York-based Citicorp, which earns most of its foreign profits from Brazil, seems slim. And so immense that just in 1982 it had to borrow $17 billion to help pay $10 billion of interest due and another $7 billion of principal.[1] His comment may not be as extreme as the words suggest. The United States owes enormous sums to its lenders and no one really expects full repayment.

Brazil's reliance on rescheduling as a solution to its debt dilemma is far from unique. The financial magazine *Euromoney* labeled 1982 "The Year of Rescheduling" and forecast more for 1983, and yet more for the following year. The magazine identified twenty countries unable to meet $28 billion in loans due—almost three times more than in 1981. "[These are] assets that will sit, or lie, on banks' balance sheets until they are rescheduled," it said. "That amount would swallow more than the combined shareholders' funds of the six largest banks in the world, and it is the highest in Euromarket history."[2]

The problem promises to get worse. MIT economist Lester Thurow suggests that the idea of a "debtor's cartel" may not be so far fetched. "In this option," he writes, "the ten largest debtors secretly get together and agree to default—all on the same day. . . . The idea is so logical that there well may be diplomats from one of the big debtors running around the Third World already trying to put such a cartel together."[3] By 1986, total Third World debt will reach the $1 trillion level, accompanied by even more onerous interest burdens. In order to tame this escalation, several conditions and initiatives will have to be made workable. First, new loans to Third World countries will have to be leveled off and even reversed. Second, austerity measures and stricter fiscal behavior will have to be accepted as conditions of further financing support. Third, world lending institutions such as the International Monetary Fund and its allied banking arms will have to shoulder a larger burden of lending—moving much of the creditor responsibility away from commercial banks and in many cases into the laps of taxpayers. And fourth, the investment community itself will have to rethink its own monitoring and management of debtor capacity—in particular in Third World cases such as Mexico, Brazil, and Argentina that account for the lion's share of overextended Western world obligations. These four measures will not come without pain. Nor will they come without continued brinksmanship between order or chaos in the world's financial marketplace.

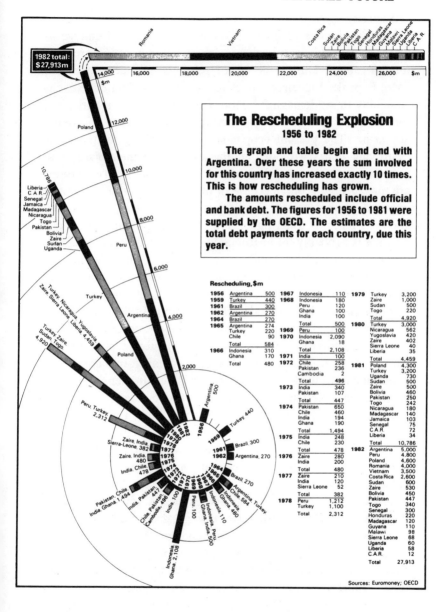

1982 total: $27,913m

The Rescheduling Explosion
1956 to 1982

The graph and table begin and end with Argentina. Over these years the sum involved for this country has increased exactly 10 times. This is how rescheduling has grown.

The amounts rescheduled include official and bank debt. The figures for 1956 to 1981 were supplied by the OECD. The estimates are the total debt payments for each country, due this year.

Rescheduling, $m

Year	Country	$m
1956	Argentina	500
1959	Turkey	440
1961	Brazil	300
1962	Argentina	270
1964	Brazil	270
1965	Argentina	274
	Turkey	220
	Chile	90
	Total	584
1966	Indonesia	310
	Ghana	170
	Total	480
1967	Indonesia	110
1968	Indonesia	180
	Peru	120
	Ghana	100
	India	100
	Total	500
1969	Peru	100
1970	Indonesia	2,090
	Ghana	18
	Total	2,108
1971	India	100
1972	Chile	258
	Pakistan	236
	Cambodia	2
	Total	496
1973	India	340
	Pakistan	107
	Total	447
1974	Pakistan	650
	Chile	460
	India	194
	Ghana	190
	Total	1,494
1975	India	248
	Chile	230
	Total	478
1976	Zaire	280
	India	200
	Total	480
1977	Zaire	210
	India	120
	Sierra Leone	52
	Total	382
1978	Peru	1,212
	Turkey	1,100
	Total	2,312
1979	Turkey	3,200
	Zaire	1,000
	Sudan	500
	Togo	220
	Total	4,920
1980	Turkey	3,000
	Nicaragua	562
	Yugoslavia	420
	Zaire	402
	Sierra Leone	40
	Liberia	35
	Total	4,459
1981	Poland	4,300
	Turkey	3,200
	Uganda	730
	Sudan	500
	Zaire	500
	Bolivia	460
	Pakistan	250
	Togo	242
	Nicaragua	180
	Madagascar	140
	Jamaica	103
	Senegal	75
	C.A.R.	72
	Liberia	34
	Total	10,786
1982	Argentina	5,000
	Peru	4,800
	Poland	4,600
	Romania	4,000
	Vietnam	3,500
	Costa Rica	2,600
	Sudan	600
	Zaire	530
	Bolivia	450
	Pakistan	447
	Togo	340
	Senegal	300
	Honduras	220
	Madagascar	120
	Guyana	110
	Malawi	98
	Sierra Leone	68
	Uganda	60
	Liberia	58
	C.A.R.	12
	Total	27,913

Sources: Euromoney; OECD

125

Austerity

The possibilities of inviting serious disorder could emerge as national growth strategies are slowed by reduced sources of foreign capital. During the fall of 1983, the president of Brazil, João Baptista Figueiredo declared before the United Nations Assembly that "demand for goods from rich nations is shrinking, foreign aid is falling, loans are drying up and obstacles to exports are rising. The present economic policy of the great powers is destroying riches without building anything in their place."⁴ In East Bloc nations such as Poland and Romania, austerity measures are manageable if only because of the strict authoritarian control imposed on the society. Despite absences of meat, staples, and goods as basic as toilet paper and soap, the potential for social uprising is probably nil in Romania and unlikely in Poland since the dismantling of the Solidarity movement by the government.

In Third World nations, however, social unrest resulting from new economic constraints could erupt from seething barrios and working class neighborhoods. The Chilean debacle that toppled Salvadore Allende was induced by an economic chaos imposed on it by U.S. efforts to stifle an infusion of Western capital into the nation. In Nicaragua and El Salvador economic forces are central determinants of those countries' political fates. In seemingly stable major Latin American powers such as Mexico, Brazil, Argentina, and Venezuela the climate for unrest will worsen. Observers of these nations, such as international business consultant George A. Hodges, Jr., suggest that "in many of these countries, and Mexico in particular, you'll probably see many more serious spontaneous demonstrations. Of those four nations, Mexico is the biggest question," he says. "While no one expects a government overthrow it is not clear to what extent social disruptions might go if their economy doesn't recover fast enough."⁵

Mexico's hopes rest on the performance of one company, Pemex, which alone contributes three-quarters of the nation's total export earnings. Its product, oil, is itself buffeted by contradictory forces. Domestic production is going up just as world prices are going down. As a result, 1982 oil revenues fell by about 15 percent despite a 20 percent rise in barrels of oil extracted. Adding to the financial confusion is a necessary new investment of $2 billion in 1983 for more wells required to maintain the higher extraction rate. All of this happens while strict austerity measures are being applied by President Miguel de la Madrid. One effect will be to reduce Mexico's gross domestic product by 3 percent; for Pemex it means a 40 percent reduction in its overall budget and a halt of construction on its fifty-story headquarters building in Mexico City. The shell of that building is emphatic testimony to the vagaries of oil wealth—or oil poverty of the 1980s. For a country sitting on financial quicksand $85 billion deep, the juggling of fates and fortunes is not enviable. To outside observers what adds fuel to the worst case predictions is a series of upheavals popularly labeled "IMF riots" which occurred a decade before when the International Monetary Fund imposed rigid economic performance standards on borrower countries. The resulting austerity and conservative fiscal guidelines unleashed political turmoil in countries as disparate as Egypt, Ghana, and Peru during late in the 1970s.

Another eventuality affecting debtor-creditor nation relations will be an intensified and perhaps more acerbic North-South debate between the industrial "have" nations and the less developed "have nots." One effect might be an emotional public countereffort in the United States to reduce foreign aid and loans and to introduce more restrictive trade terms. While such measures would ultimately hurt the U.S. economy, itself dependent on foreign exports to Third World trade partners, the cause and effect could easily be lost in a battle of accusatory rhetoric.

For the lender nations and their commercial banking institutions the issue lingers in a dangerous and misunderstood twilight of depositor confidences. Should perceptions of any single bank's fragility get out of hand because of overextended loans to foreign borrowers, the vast interlocking network of financial institutions could face an unbridgeable liquidity crisis. Recent efforts by eleven banks to shore up the collapsed reserves of Seafirst Corporation in Seattle is one indication of the sensitivity of fellow lenders to maintaining confidence among depositors. In the international world of finance such crisis consortia can be expected

127

from central banks of various nations. What all bankers fear—and assiduously avoid talking about publicly—is the run on one bank that sets off a global tidal wave. Anthony Sampson, author of *The Money Lenders,* recalled: "It has always been possible for a country in difficulties to bankrupt a bank, as Britain had brought down the Medicis, or Argentina had brought down Barings." All too aware that history's lessons are there to be repeated, bankers aggressively cultivate public perceptions of a steady and optimistic future for world banking. Thomas C. Theobald, Citicorp's vice-chairman, states: "There isn't any statistical evidence to say we're in a period of more pressure and more and more strain than at any other time." At Bank of America, Richard Puz, a vice-president says: "The news is not good, but the banks are strong."[6]

But the bankers do worry. Frequent meetings are held to tackle a problem that appears far less solvable than the press releases admit. Third World debt has soared fivefold to $500 billion between 1973 and 1982, plus $100 billion more in interest charges; East Bloc debt has risen tenfold during the same period to a high of about $90 billion plus interest. Of these amounts the proportion owed to commercial lending banks reached two-thirds the total—up from less than half less than ten years before—or about $370 billion of commercial bank money at risk. And while much of this debt may not be fairly categorized as unpayable, there is great concern that a mix of a single default, coupled with unpredictable political events, might undermine the world's inverted financial pyramid. Under such conditions what is the likelihood of managing Third World debt without inviting unrest? What initiatives are already visible in meeting these goals?

Send in the Managers

In a variation of the crisis management method of restructuring a potential corporate failure, three major international investment brokers created a debt and insolvency advisory committee. Introduced in Chapter 7, the troika brings together investment experience from three financial capitals. The three—Lehman Brothers Kuhn Loeb, Maison Lazard, and S.G. Warburg—came into being when invited to repair the $10 billion demise of

Indonesia's giant Pertamina oil company in 1975. Since then a long list of indebted country clients has accumulated. The fees from such nations as Costa Rica, Zaire, Turkey, and a number of West African countries are large. Six months of advice can bring in $0.5 million to $1 million. In return, the advisors provide counsel during rescheduling negotiations, help prepare detailed debt audits, or perform many information-gathering tasks normally undertaken by a financial ministry. "Everyone's trying to get into the business," the *International Herald Tribune* quoted a British banker as saying. "It's a status business. You're not just peddling junk bonds," another commented. The bankers' incentive is large, risk-free fees.

But the profitability of this advisory sideline is attracting not only competitors but pointed criticism. "Some World Bank and IMF officials," says *Euromoney* magazine, "complain that the merchant banks are creaming off large fees by recycling second-hand statistics and superfluous advice." Despite the more obvious concerns that such services may be overpriced and even too narrowly self-serving to the advisor's own possible associated lending interests, the value of a roving advisory financial task force has substantial merit. Since such a group can function independently of the IMF and its own political priorities or of any formal external institutions, it can advise with greater latitude. Also, it can perform highly specialized tasks that only arise within the feverish deadlines of looming loan defaults.

Such professional counsel, if properly insulated from the lender institutions' self-interest, could become a condition for subsequent loans. This would not only infuse professional judgment into borrower country evaluations of future debt capacity but would also aid in setting higher standards of information gathering and in monitoring economic performance. Its function would be styled on conditional restraints imposed by Felix Rohatyn's Municipal Assistance Corporation in New York City and a more direct managerial function akin to Victor Palmieri's crisis team. Merit is found in the troika's efforts on behalf of its own clientele, such as Costa Rica. The potentially beneficial role of a new generation of advisory bankers is seen by some financial specialists as a vitally important transfer of technology. "This is one of the most encouraging developments of recent years," says the prestigious French Institute for International Relations.[7]

More controversial are a variety of recommendations that strict restraints be placed on nations borrowing central bank capital or commercial bank debt that is directly or indirectly supported by central banks. Third World debtors see such measures as another step toward lost sovereignty in a North-South economic battle between Davids and Goliaths.

The U.S. Federal Reserve's Paul A. Volcker would like to see the IMF ensure that limits be set on amounts of money lent by commercial banks to debtor nations. Such a suggestion would turn the IMF into a far more effective world banking institution—one that its founders had envisioned at its inception four decades earlier. It would force the institution to play a far more important role in determining national policy priorities and in determining the allocation of funds to debtors. Few on the borrowing side welcome the implied intrusion of an established institution dominated more heavily than before by the industrial lender countries.

WHO'S WHO

International Monetary Fund (Washington, D.C.)
A 146-country-member organization established in 1944 to intervene in leveling imbalances in foreign exchange rates. Its primary asset is a capital fund from which loans are made to credit-squeezed nations. In February 1983, its assets were raised nearly 50 percent to $100 billion by major industrial member states.

General Arrangements to Borrow
Agreement by the "Group of Ten" leading industrial nations to support capital needs of the IMF.

World Bank (Washington, D.C.)
A creation of the 1944 Bretton Woods conference, the bank was given the mandate of financing single projects in Third World client countries facing short-term development problems. Its country "owners" total 142. The United States holds about 20 percent of its voting power. From its inception until 1982, about $100 billion was loaned by the bank and its affiliate, the International Development Association, created in 1960. Of this amount about $69 billion was outstanding at the end of 1981. Bank lending is limited to the amount of its capital. The bank has another affiliate, the International Finance Corporation which, with 122 members, focuses its resources on private sector projects.

International Bank for Reconstruction and Development
The official name of the World Bank.

Central Banks
National banks of sovereign states.

Bank for International Settlements (Basel)
A Swiss-based bank established to provide emergency credit as needed on a country-by-country basis. Its loans aid in shoring up short-term cash requirements of 60- to 90-day duration of central banks. Run by a board of twenty-nine central bank representatives.

The Institute of International Finance, Inc. (Washington, D.C.)
A U.S.-based nonprofit group established in January 1983 to provide member commercial banks with timely data on borrower country credit worthiness and to act as a borrower country forum on economic planning and objectives.

Commercial banks
Private banks with highly flexible lending policies. Most can lend up to twenty times the amount of their own deposited funds. They are located in five principal areas—New York, London, Zurich, Luxemburg, Paris, and the Bahamas and Cayman Islands—and two secondary ones in Tokyo and Frankfurt. New centers commonly called "off-shores" are growing in Hong Kong, Singapore, and Bahrain.

In the United States, the American Bankers Association has a membership of 13,000 domestic commercial banks.

The Bretton Woods Legacy

During the most crucial year of World War II, 1944, world leaders met in the mountainous and remote wooded seclusion of Bretton Woods, New Hampshire. Their deliberations focused on the need for a postwar international monetary system. Two institutions were born of this meeting: the International Monetary Fund (IMF) and the International Bank for Reconstruction and Development, better known as the World Bank. Both were intended to be on emergency call to provide short-term balance of deficit financing where needed in the case of the IMF or project-by-project support for developing countries in the case of the World Bank.

But time has taken a toll on these institutions' general mandates. The IMF's requirement of "firm surveillance" over worldwide exchange rate policies increasingly narrowed itself to countries with foreign exchange deficits—most of those being Third World nations with long-term economic problems. For the

IMF, the unwillingness of the United States to be liable to its directives was fatal to its mandate. The World Bank, on the other hand, while highly successful in becoming the best-managed lender to Third World nations, found itself increasingly at loggerheads with an uncooperative U.S. Congress and chief executive. Ronald Reagan came into office showing little enthusiasm for the institution—an attitude that would only help fuel tensions between Western and Third World nations.

At the heart of the problem was a world financial crisis that called for long-term solutions but could only turn to institutional mechanisms that were designed to provide short-term support. That urgency was called for in reevaluating their roles and powers was dramatized by the huge debt burdens of Brazil, Mexico, Argentina, and a few other big debtor nations. The fragility of their economies is leading some specialists to argue for an entirely new international financial institution—one that could assume a large part of the commercial debt backed by government guarantees. At present, however, more attention is focused on patching up the short-term effectiveness of existing institutions and less on rethinking the broad international economic edifice.

One Solution: Pay Off Debt with More Debt

One proposal is to increase the IMF's lending capacity by allowing it to add to government capital sources by borrowing directly from commercial banks. This approach is strongly resisted by the fund's managing director, Jacques de Larosière. Commercial banks are not keen on adding to their already strained commitment to financing both Third World and East Bloc debt. As lending policy debates intensify within the IMF a new factor will have to be considered. The rise of Saudi Arabia as a supplier of resources to the fund has positioned it as the sixth largest "shareholder" in the IMF. The impact of its views has yet to be fully clarified: Will it argue the Third World case or fall into line with the industrialized? The downturn of oil prices is working, at present, to mitigate a strong policymaking stance by the Saudis.

The World Bank has also reached an acute crossroads in its evolution. After thirteen years of leadership by Robert McNamara the bank became the world's leading activist institution in financing and guiding Third World development strategies. During this period loans from the bank and another lending arm, the International Development Association (IDA) surged 1,190 percent to $12.3 billion. But the mushrooming of the bank's participation in other nations' growth also spurred the ballooning of a banking bureaucracy of 2,500 employees that proved less flexible in its own views.

Alden W. Clausen, president of the bank since 1981, must resolve not only questions of internal management through possible decentralization but also ripening conflicts between U.S. pressure for more leverage over loan policies and Third World recalcitrance at such interference—a position hardened after IMF refusals to provide funds to Chile during the Allende period. In addition, the World Bank's strict lending rules—that is, that they be applied to specific rentable projects and not to finance foreign exchange needs or nonproductive resources such as military purchases—is a source of contention between the borrowers who want simple transfers of resources and old-line purists who see the bank solely as a financier of well-monitored and managed projects. The merit of the latter position is reinforced by the bank's need to finance its own lending from loans it negotiates for its fund from national or international markets at going rates.

The crisis of debt in 1982 and 1983 forced the hand of many government leaders—most significantly that of President Reagan. With commercial lending to major debtor nations leveling off and defaults looming catastrophically on the horizon, the pressure to act took precedence.

Harold Lever, an ex-cabinet minister and economic advisor to Prime Ministers Harold Wilson and James Callaghan, is an outspoken critic of this tardy governmental effort. "It was in the highest degree dangerous," he states, "that governments failed to accept collectively the commitments and responsibilities that would have both supported and disciplined the activities of the [private] banks. They must now belatedly and comprehensively repair their error—and fast."[8]

Shuttling between financial capitals in Europe and the United

States, twenty-two ministers of finance, the fund's governing board, would finally conclude that short-term remedies could only be found by issuing more debt to cover existing debt. In short, the IMF would need more government commitments to build up its loanable funds. In Washington, on February 11, 1983, they agreed that almost $32 billion had to be added, thereby increasing the fund's assets to almost $100 billion. This 47 percent increase would satisfy a refusal to go along with a far larger increase argued by European members, Japan, Canada, and Third World members of the 146-nation group. Secretary of the treasury, Donald T. Regan, would rationalize the agreement by stating: "Our recovery and the recovery of other nations are tied together. The nations now in debt represent customers for our exports. . . . These quota increases are sufficient for the foreseeable future," he added optimistically.[9]

An additional signal of the severity of the liquidity crisis was underscored by a parallel decision of the world's ten leading industrial powers to create an emergency fund of $20 billion. This Group of Ten commitment tripled an earlier decision to make additional emergency loan capital available to the IMF.

Whether more debt can indeed solve the problem of current debt and default is open to debate. One thing is perfectly clear: The emergency refinancing of the IMF's assets only defers to the future a reform of the world financial system. In its 1982 report on *The State of the World Economy,* the French Institute for International Relations concludes that the global economic crisis is a "crisis of economic management." The system is in a state of disequilibrium. This was induced by "static" from inflation, unemployment, and financial distortions. The report turns to the writings of Jacques Attali—now a Mitterrand counselor—to explain that "in nature there are situations in which phenomena starting as outside interferences [or static] become transformed into the determinants of the system, leaving the information signals that once gave the system its shape to become the external interference." This proposition leads the institute to two alternative conclusions. One is that a new international management system will eliminate the current static; the other is that the static will prevail and become institutionalized in a world in which national governments are impotent to deal with the stresses of economic disequilibrium.

The Mirror Game Solution

To an outsider looking into the global business of lending, the revelations take on an Alice in Wonderland quality. A game of mirror magic—now you see it now you don't—is being played that brings into question the professional credibility of banking institutions. Philippe Simonnot, a French journalist, explained the new abracadabra. "The banks," he wrote, "lend just enough new money to allow debtor countries to remain current on their interest payments. Put into other words, *the banks are paying themselves* [emphasis added]. One is thrust into a grand illusion. But the banks quite prefer the 'optical illusion' to a firm and final declaration of bankruptcy."[10] To declare the reality would only "lead to a loss of confidence by depositors and shareholders," he concludes.

A signal that ad hoc confidence-building measures were urgently needed to account for the unmanageable complexity of world debt was evidenced in a decision by international bankers from the Americas, Europe, and Japan to create a monitoring institute to track the sinuous web of outstanding debt obligations. The creation of the Institute of International Finance, Inc., in January 1983, was instigated at the urging of the Chase Manhattan Bank's William S. Ogden.

Leading commercial banks from nine industrial nations (see note below for a list of the founding members) agreed to found and finance the activities of the new nonprofit institute. The new

Note: Founding member banks (January 11, 1983)
BRAZIL: Banco Brasiliero de Descontos, S.A.; Banco Itau, S.A.; Banco Real, S.A.
CANADA: Bank of Nova Scotia; Bank of Montreal; Canadian Imperial Bank of Commerce; The Royal Bank of Canada
FRANCE: Banque Nationale de Paris; Crédit Lyonnais
WEST GERMANY: Commerzbank, A.G.; Dresdner Bank, A.G.; West Deutsche Landesbank, A.G.
ITALY: Banca Nazionale del Lavoro; Banco de Roma

organization was born on January 11, a result of preparatory meetings held during the prior year. Briefing materials on the new institute suggest two primary functions for the anticipated three- to fifty-person Washington-based staff. The first is to collect and disseminate information of use to member banks in making lending decisions to borrowing nations. The second is to offer a forum in which a borrowing country can discuss and develop economic plans and projections.

The thirty-six founding members' unstated motive for creating this ad hoc institute stems from a belief that confidence in commercial bank international lending had eroded and needed quick repair. One reason for the loss of confidence, as Werner Stange, a senior vice-president of Morgan Guaranty Trust Company suggests, "is a common statement heard that there is a lot of name lending involved in a bank's decision to lend to a country. Many banks will follow automatically by saying 'If they are in, I'll follow.' As a result, during the peak of the Eurodollar days, indepth analysis was not done by many as deeply as it should have."[11] This view is echoed by Paul Sacks, a partner in a risk consulting firm, Multinational Strategies. He states: "Congress, regulators and the media want to know how lending decisions are made, and the banks will have to present systems that are defensible." To date, he says, too much of the decisionmaking of credit risk is based on what he terms a "caste society" in which the line executives are the Brahmins and the professional analysts are the untouchables. "There is no state of the art," he argues.[12]

A second reason is more subtle. The leading U.S. international

JAPAN: The Bank of Tokyo, LTD.; Dai-Ichi Kangyo Bank; Industrial Bank of Japan; The Mitsubishi Bank, Limited
SWITZERLAND: Crédit Suisse; Swiss Bank Corporation; Union Bank of Switzerland
UNITED KINGDOM: Barclays Bank International Ltd.; Lloyds Bank International; Midland Bank PLC; National Westminster Bank
UNITED STATES: Bank of America, N.S.T.A.; Bankers Trust Company; Chemical Bank; Citibank, N.A.; Continental Illinois National Bank & Trust Company; The First National Bank of Chicago; Manufacturers Hanover Trust Co., Mellon Bank; Morgan Guaranty Trust Company of New York; The Chase Manhattan Bank, N.A.

banks collect about 40 percent of their loanable funds from domestic sources—a vast sum that it cannot afford to jeopardize. Much of this capital is provided by regional banks which, it is feared, might pull back because of the widely reported uncertainty of the repayment capacity of debtor nations. The institute is intended in part, according to news reports,[13] to provide these regionals with their own information resource on which to make future lending judgments.

What problems in the normal credit-risk analysis might be remedied by the creation of the institute? "Most of all," says Stange, "is that timely information can be provided." Often the most current data are six months old at best and in many cases by the time it has filtered through intermediaries such as the Bank for International Settlements in Basel the data can be a year old. In addition, much of the useful current data needed to make credit evaluation is held by central banks—or in the United States by the Federal Reserve—and not shared with commercial banks. The institute expects to overcome both of these deficiencies by putting its own analysts to work. To make its judgment more pertinent, frequent forays or missions to borrower nations will add a depth of understanding that can only come from being there.

The bottom line so frequently lost in cursory credit analyses is a single issue: Can a country service its debt obligations from exports? "Up to now," says Stange, "much of the rationale for lending was based on the potential value of national reserves or on the national resource endowment. An overemphasis on these aspects forgot the more important point of whether an export-based cash flow analysis could demonstrate an ability to service the debt."

In an international financial world in which confidence is the most critical factor in the stability of the whole system, the institute's anticipated functions and implicit beliefs are expectedly bullish. Debt will be honored, its members believe. The only problem is to keep all of the banks in, and that means confidence building. Beyond the short-term question of rescheduling the immense mountain of accumulated debt, which the institute is not equipped to solve, the focus of its efforts is on a future financial environment that "can tame the euphoria of overlending that carried lenders away in the seventies," says Stange.[14] Dissemination of timely and accurate data is seen as a crucial step in ameliorating such passions.

INFORMALITY THAT WORKS: The Paris Club

The club's informal, staffless, and officeless group of international central bankers aid debtor nations in rescheduling official—not commercial—debt payments. In operation since 1956, it acts only after an agreement on a recovery program has been reached between a given country and the IMF. Deliberations are held to a two-day period. The country's creditors are invited to a meeting with the club. Those who appear agree to general rescheduling terms suggested by the club and to specific loan terms in direct negotiations with the debtor country. The intention of the group is to provide a mechanism for efficiently determined short-term solutions. The central figure of the club is Michel Camdessus, a high official of the French Treasury who brokers the informal negotiations. "We represent creditors," he says, "and not aid donors. There are other ways of granting aid."[15]

In 1981, the Central African Republic, Liberia, Madagascar, Pakistan, Senegal, Togo, Uganda, and Zaire rescheduled their debt through the Paris Club.

INFORMALITY THAT TERRIFIES: The Eurodollar market:

"Terror approaches panic when one imagines the tens of billions of speculative dollars that can be instantly flung across the world like an unshackled cargo in the hold of a sinking ship."[16]

Doing the Unthinkable

Earlier mention was made of Lester Thurow's speculation that it would not be unthinkable to imagine a debtor's cartel drawing the primary big borrowers together and deciding en masse to default. Chrysler threatened to do it and got more than $1 billion in guaranteed money from the federal government. AEG-Telefunken did it in Germany and managed to get even more debt issued to it from its lenders. The Third World option to default— an absolute reverse scenario of the OPEC cartel—would instantly shatter the placid image of confidence exuded by world bankers. Not only would the leading commercial bankers be thrown into declaring immediate bankruptcy, but a web of secondary and tertiary partners in the financial grapevine would suffer equal fates. The obvious effect would be to force central banks into the breach to support these institutions with taxpayer funds. Again Thurow: "It would be far better, however, if the central bankers announced their intentions to do so before, rather than after, any default. Prevention is always better than remediation."[17]

One remedy in such a scenario would be to declare a debtor's holiday in which parts of principal and interest obligations are forgiven by commercial lenders with a guarantee by their central banks that the losses incurred would be instantaneously covered. In this manner institutional bankruptcies could be avoided and borrower obligations could be brought back to manageable sums. To Third World nations this could be viewed positively as the transfer of wealth from richer to poorer that they so heatedly prescribe. In an ideal world environment in which such a masterstroke could be envisioned, the participation of the IMF as a monitor of future Third World economic performance would be an essential ingredient. This would create a hybrid form of the Municipal Assistance Corporation as befits a global economy— and who better to consider at the helm but a Felix Rohatyn.

In another twist of the same outcome, an investment banker at Lehman Brothers Kuhn Loeb Incorporated in New York, Jeffrey Garten, has suggested a debtor's holiday by arguing for the creation of a "discount facility" allowing creditor nations to pay "70 cents now on a dollar owed later" in order to relieve debt pressure.[18] An ex-deputy director of the State Department's policy planning staff, Garten is emphatic in calling for a government-initiated solution. "War, it is said, is too important to leave to the generals," he writes. "Can the responsibility for insuring global financial security be left to the bankers?"[19]

A more aggressive posturing of central banks has been discussed for a long time. Early in the 1970s a committee of financial experts formed a group they labeled the Shadow Open Market Committee. They see the Achilles heel of the world's financial system in uncontrolled financial centers such as Luxembourg and the Cayman Islands, where no central banks exist. To date, their call for an international understanding between central banks on emergency measures to be taken—when and if large banks fail— remains unheeded.[20]

Chapter 9

IN SEARCH OF DISCIPLINE

L ENDING REACHED an inglorious high during the 1970s; the price must now be paid, and the implications are far from comforting. By the summer of 1983, renewed warnings of potential collapse of the world banking system reached the public. Both the National Security Council and the Central Intelligence Agency, in opinions running counter to prevailing White House attitudes, forecast that, even under the most optimistic economic recovery conditions, most Third World debtors would not be able to meet their debt obligations. Brazil, with $5 billion in emergency credit rapidly spent, asked for more. An estimated $3 to $4 billion more was needed to keep it afloat in 1983. Once-rich Nigeria ran out of foreign currency reserves and announced its inability to pay $3.3 billion in overdue short-term payments. A Latin American journalist, Carlos Rangel, said of Venezuela's dire financial condition, "they feel as if a trap door had opened under their feet."

Adding to the mounting concern felt in world financial centers, ministries, and bank boardrooms worldwide is the recognition that all of this has happened before—and with calamitous results. Following World War I, the United States became a primary lender to both European and Latin American nations. In a foreboding precedent to today's crisis, Mexico was one of the largest borrowers. In a depression era book entitled *Mexico and Her Foreign Creditors,* its author, Columbia University economist Edgar Turlington, calculated that in 1930 Mexico's indebtedness totaled $1 billion, a third of which accumulated in unpaid interest. The debt had become so large that by the end of the 1920s few could honor their obligations. Already, during the prior thirty-six months, several major international debt rescheduling agreements had been negotiated. Then Bolivia defaulted in December 1930 and the roof caved in. Several countries followed in rapid sequence: Peru, Chile, Brazil, and Uruguay. Within three years, with the exception of Argentina and Haiti, all Latin American debt was in default. Little of it was ever paid.

In an uncanny parallel to the confidence expressed in recent years by bankers and government officials that countries like Mexico can afford their debt, Turlington wrote confidently of Mexico's ability to pay its debts. While acknowledging that a large population of very poor laborers had little taxable property to generate income for the government, he reminded his readers that Mexico's "enormous potential wealth" would ultimately help to service the existing debt. He could not have been more wrong. Much of that debt was never repaid. Yet his argument is used again today to rationalize further loans to Mexico, Brazil, and others.

From his supply side ideological perch, President Reagan stood fast on predictions of a coming global industrial recovery. His solution to the world debt crisis, as a result, was no more complex than waiting for better times. A major hurdle in this optimistic expectation are the $200 billion a year—or more—federal budgetary deficits. To a worried IMF this is the principal barrier to both a U.S. and a world economic recovery. Meanwhile, an informally organized group of 300 business leaders from the United States, Japan, and Europe—the Trilateral Commission—urged continued lending by commercial banks to Third World nations on the condition that strict austerity measures accompany the receipt of loans. This approach, voiced by the group's spokesman and former World Bank president, Robert McNamara, considered the "world debt crisis as non-existent." Yet critics, even among the members, saw the Trilateral Commission's position as far too conventional in its prescriptions for a problem expected to get far worse and far more burdensome.

Lying low and lending more may be the quickest route to

disaster. International financial stability is subject to innumerable pressures, any one of which can cause immense disruption. The balancing game between chaos and order in a contemporary world of uncontrolled exchange rates, of Eurodollar markets that are subject to no single authority, of national fiscal and monetary policies that are rarely coordinated, and of international institutions with little political leverage is a delicate filigree of interdependent relationships at best. Discussing the dynamics of contemporary world economic relations, Albert Bressand suggests that "to no small extent, the difficulties we are presently going through and the vulnerabilities we have developed reflect a crisis of ignorance. We called for a worldeconomy. Now we have it. The time has come to learn how to make productive use of it, lest we become the victims of our creation."[1]

The tensions caused by Third World national debt illustrate the problem defined by Bressand. Nations and their corporate subjects have indeed forged a new "worldeconomy" in which national barriers and boundaries have lost meaning and in which economic events can no longer be insulated as domestic. It is now possible to conceive of a national default by one or a group of nations on their foreign debt as a catalyst for what a U.S. government economist termed a truly "explosive thing." Rioting in São Paulo, Brazil, in the spring of 1983 was the first signal of pressures reaching the boiling point in economically strained developing countries. If allowed to get out of hand, such crises could lead the world economic order into uncontrollable financial convulsions from which few might emerge unscathed.

Paradoxically, the originators of this new international economy are the same ones who show great reluctance to invent new rules adapted to the competitive environment. Bankers—many profiting from their own allegiance to, and stimulation of, the new worldeconomy—would be the worst offenders. Most would lend freely to all comers with the argument that they alone were keeping the worldeconomy afloat by helping to recycle a barrage of new OPEC profits. Yet all of them would quickly retreat to the safety of their own national central banks to find refuge from

potential insolvencies and default by numerous national borrowers. Their behavior epitomized the schizophrenia of lending under
one set of rules and calling in the loans under another.

The unfolding sequence of giant corporate failures starting in
1970, to New York City's failure in 1975, to immense national
defaults in 1980 are in retrospect the logical outcome of unre-
strained lending by American and foreign financiers. Without a
central financial arbiter, the process took on a life of its own. The
global business of debt found itself without rules or restraints.
"Our first duty," Bressand writes, "is to acknowledge how little
we know. Our second is to close the widening gap between
growing interdependence and declining collective capacity to deal
with the perils it brings."[2]

It now seems clear that the easily incurred indebtedness of the
Penn Central—and many other corporations to follow in its
footsteps—or of New York City, and then Poland, Mexico,
Argentina, and Korea led to its logical extreme. Lending and
borrowing without oversight ran headlong toward default and
insolvency. Both creditors and debtors were at fault; the first for
not protecting their assets more rigorously and allowing public
institutions ultimately to bear the risk at taxpayer expense; the
second for extending the asking hand with far too little concern for
how the indebtedness would be managed. In the corporate
environment such excesses quickly led to bankruptcy—and in
some cases to outright liquidation of the indebted firms. In
overextended country cases, the debt lingers.

With such a sadly mismanaged decade as a backdrop, what is
even more shocking is the blatancy of the Reagan administration
in pushing the indebtedness of the United States to unprecedented
depths. While arguing fiscal conservatism and a balanced budget,
Reagan has wagered on the correctness of a policy to finance a
menu of exotic defense technologies with immense budgetary
deficits. If untamed by Congress, these will accumulate unabated
to the trillion-dollar level within a few years. Such financial
extremism will only release another round of high interest rate
policies with constraining effects on national economies throughout the globe. Another basis for economic collapse could easily

ensue, dragging the world into a far deeper and far more pervasive depression than that experienced during the 1930s.

What might be learned from a decade of domestic American experience in managing debt and bankruptcy both in the corporate environment and in unique cases such as the New York City crisis? And what lessons might be applied to the threatening signs of default by Third World nations?

A new generation of bankruptcy professionals, catapulted into public prominence by the Penn Central and New York City crises, introduced two new tactical skills. The first was the art of managing bankrupt entities back to health. Victor Palmieri's or Felix Rohatyn's talents, and those of a variety of other turnaround specialists, perfected the art of crisis management. Penn Central, which had been given up as lost by its own executives and by outside consultants, or New York City, which was viewed as so entangled in its own fiscal problems that nothing other than absolute failure could possibly result, were demonstrated not to be victims of terminal cancer but of mismanagement. The new experts were able to reinfuse order and vitality. This lesson was eventually taken up by investment banking houses. They started selling similar skills to indebted Third World countries.

A second important outcome of the 1970s was Edward Altman's art of predicting failure. His Z or Zeta factor had the valuable potential of providing the shareholder, corporate director, employee, loan officer, or investment analyst with a predictive device to forewarn of danger and to stimulate immediate corrective actions. Altman's model, translated into federal legislation, could require immediate notification of shareholders, creditors, employees, or others, that a corporation was in danger. Much like a warning label on a cigarette package, a disclosure would be required announcing that x corporation was "dangerous to your economic health." Such a warning, appropriately phrased and reported in quarterly Securities and Exchange Commission filings or in corporate annual statements, would trigger a call for a board of directors to act with all due expediency to repair the damage. A "Corporate Trigger Act" would be controversial if only because many might view it as an unnecessary intrusion of government into corporate life. Yet, if the intrusion were only to require disclosure of problematic corporate indebtedness—much as car markers are required to announce product defects and recall cars for repairs— the unprotected long-term interests of shareholder and creditor could be served to far greater advantage.

The American experience with the management and prediction of bankruptcy—and the suggested "triggering" warnings—has direct bearing on how one might resolve the far more risky and far more threatening problem of Third World indebtedness. The question to be asked by commercial banks, the lenders, and national central banks—the ultimate arbitrators—is whether these skills and the conceptual tools now incorporated into U.S. bankruptcy laws are indeed applicable to a settlement of the world debt situation.

The guiding legal concept is the "second-chance" provision now widely accepted as a basic principle underlying any settlement with a debtor in bankruptcy proceedings. It recognizes a debtor's ability to pay only a portion of an outstanding obligation to a creditor. Once a settlement is agreed upon, the debtor is free to start a new life unfettered by further claims or obligations. Such a rule, applied to many Third World nations hopelessly buried in too easily issued and too easily accepted debt, would provide an immense stimulus to the global economy by restoring a new atmosphere of partnership and shared responsibility between North and South nations—a geographic distinction characterized by the industrialized lenders, predominantly in the Northern Hemisphere, and the less developed borrowers, predominantly in the Southern Hemisphere.

Should such a basis for settlement be considered by commercial and central banks of lending nations, the amounts in question and the formula for agreement could be negotiated under the auspices of a neutral ad hoc organization such as the Paris Club, already well versed in helping Third World nations to reschedule their debt. An oversimplified example of how the debt might be reduced to manageable amounts is an across-the-board reduction of debt and interest by 10, 25, or 35 percent. A 10 percent reduction of the $600 billion in outstanding Third World debt translates to about $60 billion. The burden, if accepted by leading lender country central banks with national parliamentary approval, could be borne with far less difficulty and at far less cost than if the existing debt burdens were left unattended. Thus, if the United States, Japan, France, Germany, England, or Switzerland were to concur, the resulting proportional share to Americans might total $10 to $15 billion—a price far outweighed by the renewed economic stability and confidence of Third World trade partners.

Beyond the second-chance principle is the more practical application of crisis management skills to the financial ministries of many Third World debtor nations. A new kind of foreign aid and knowledge transfer might come in the form of highly professional and experienced economic managers—administered by the IMF or World Bank—whose task would be to introduce appropriate management and planning technologies into national financial ministries, much as happened in the New York City case. Acceptance of such professional advice should be made conditional on a lowering of the debt obligation and in the future should be triggered by any crisis that a "national Zeta model" might forecast. A combination of reduced debt obligations, a fresh start with crisis management reforms, and neutral measures of performance that could anticipate debt crises would aid immeasurably in restoring confidence and collaboration to the worldeconomy.

One step toward achieving these goals is for commercial bankers and central banks to meet in a historic session with the purpose of agreeing to a second-chance settlement for an overburdened Third World. One might call it the "Global Debt Conference." Whenever or wherever it is held, its purpose would be (1) to resolve the legacy of the financiers' decade and to restore a collaborative partnership between the more and the less developed nations of the non-Communist world and (2) to forge new agreements on the institutional oversight necessary to ensure future stability. To date, though, the will to tackle the looming Third World insolvency is still focused on deferring the real issue of repayment or settlement. An attempt to reach consensus among the major industrialized nations at the May 1983 summit meeting in Williamsburg produced only the broadest expression of "concern" and an agreement that more lending was necessary. A far bigger step toward a solution is needed.

It was just a hundred years ago in the United States that Jay L. Torrey, as a young St. Louis lawyer, started his campaign to get America to accept its first bankruptcy law at a time when the absence of a law was creating a domestic economic crisis similar to the world crisis we now face. To make his case before numerous audiences he used the imagery of a wrecked ship at sea in a storm. As quoted in an earlier chapter, he said then of the depressed U.S. economy: "She can be saved only by cutting away the wreckage. That relief is what the absence of a bankruptcy law denies to the businessman overtaken by a storm of disaster." A hundred years later, Albert Bressand argued with a similar nautical flourish: "National decision-makers are revealed as sailors on an open sea, taking the utmost care to adhere to the course of their choosing when in fact the currents, winds and swirls are often carrying them in the opposite direction."[3] Bringing them back into the mainstream means changing the course and ridding the vessel of unneeded ballast.

Not to adapt, not to act with dispatch, will be to transfer the burden to the average citizen, who bears the ultimate price of austerity budgets, collapsed economies, and weakened trade partnerships. Those risks belong to no single nation. Rather, they belong to all.

NOTES

Introduction

1. "Debt Burdens Take Big Toll of Businesses," *New York Times,* October 4, 1982.

Chapter 1

1. "Crumbling Credits," *Wall Street Journal,* July 30, 1982.
2. *World Financial Markets,* October 1982, p. 2.
3. "Confronting Global Financial Insecurity," *New York Times,* December 9, 1982.
4. "Debt's New Dangers," *Business Week,* July 26, 1982.
5. "West Europe Besieged by Bankruptcies," *Christian Science Monitor,* August 12, 1982.
6. *Across the Board,* May 5, 1982, p. 3.
7. "Brazilian Condemns Liberalization Foes," *New York Times,* April 11, 1983.

Chapter 2

1. "Woman Joins Panel of Bankruptcy Judges," *New York Times,* September 7, 1983.
2. "Uniform System of Bankruptcy," 55th Congress, 2nd Session, House Report #65, Washington, D.C., 1896, p. 47.
3. William Hotchkiss, *North American Review,* April 1901.
4. "Bankruptcy in the United States," *The Nation,* December 16, 1897.
5. Charles Warren, *Bankruptcy in U.S. History,* Harvard University Press, Cambridge, Mass., 1935, p. 22.
6. Ibid., p. 25.
7. Ibid., p. 56.
8. Ibid., p. 107.
9. Ibid., p. 122.
10. Ibid.
11. Ibid., p. 136.
12. Ibid., p. 16.
13. Ibid., p. 4; see Clause 4 of Section 8 of Article I.
14. "The Torrey Bankruptcy Bill," 54th Congress, 1st Session, Senate Document #237, 1896.
15. Ibid.
16. *North American Review,* April 1901.
17. Ibid.

18. From *Industrial Distributor,* May 1981, as excerpted from the National Association of Credit Management's *Credit Manual of Commercial Laws.*

Chapter 3

1. "European Linked to Illegal Acts Shielded by C.I.A.," *New York Times,* February 8, 1983.
2. Joseph R. Daughen and Peter Binzen, *The Wreck of the Penn Central,* Little, Brown and Company, Boston, 1971, p. 264.
3. "Are More Chryslers in the Offing?" *Forbes,* February 2, 1981, p. 69.
4. "Sorting Out the Saxon Tangle," *New York Times,* July 15, 1982.
5. *Forbes,* February 2, 1981.
6. "Bankruptcy Wave," *Wall Street Journal,* May 24, 1981, p. 1.
7. "International Harvester - Can It Survive the Banks' Move In?" *Business Week,* June 22, 1981, p. 66.
8. "People Behind Penn Square," *New York Times,* September 16, 1982.
9. "Continental Discloses Poor Loans," *New York Times,* August 4, 1982.
10. *Small Business Report,* August 1982, p. 5.

Chapter 4

1. Interview with the author, September 15, 1982.
2. Securities and Exchange Commission Staff Report, Subcommittee on Economic Stabilization, Committee on Banking, Finance and Urban Affairs, House of Representatives, 95th Congress, First Session, *Transactions in Securities of the City of New York,* Government Printing Office, Washington, D.C., 1977, Ch. 1, p. 3.
3. "New York Is Still on the Brink," *Fortune,* July 1977.
4. "Capital Needs and Priorities for the City of New York," The New York City Planning Commission, New York, 1981, p 15.
5. Subcommittee on Economic Stabilization, Ch. 1, p. 6.
6. Jeremy Bernstein, "Allocating Sacrifice," *New Yorker,* January 24, 1983.
7. "Does New York's Municipal Crisis Mean Bankruptcy?" *Financial World,* January 1, 1975.
8. *Business Week,* June 2, 1975, p. 52.
9. Jeremy Bernstein, "Allocating Sacrifice."
10. Subcommittee on Economic Stabilization, Ch. 1, p. 14.
11. *Business Week,* June 2, 1975, p. 52.
12. *Newsweek,* August 2, 1982.
13. Subcommittee on Economic Stabilization, p. III.
14. Ibid., Ch. 1, p. 7.

15. Ibid., Ch. 1, p. 257.
16. Ibid., Ch. 4, p. 3.
17. Ibid., Ch. 4, p. 25.
18. Ibid., Ch. 4, p. 37.
19. Ibid., Ch. 4, p. 73.

Chapter 5

1. "We Cannot Create a Municipal Assistance Corporation for Poland. Let It Go Bankrupt," *New York Times,* January 1, 1982.
2. "Les Dettes de l'Est et du Tiers Monde," *Le Temps Stratégique,* Summer 1982, p. 59.
3. French Institute for International Relations (IFRI), *RAMSES 1982: The State of the World Economy,* Ballinger Publishing Company, Cambridge, Mass., 1982, p. 144.
4. "Mexican Crisis is Seen Forcing Oil Output Up," *New York Times,* August 26, 1982.
5. Interview with the author, September 17, 1982.
6. IFRI, p. 135.
7. "International Banking's House of Cards," *New York Times,* October 24, 1982.
8. Interview with the author, February 1983.
9. IFRI, p. 134.
10. Ibid., p. 135.
11. *New York Times,* January 11, 1982.
12. "Aid Urged for Poor Countries," *New York Times,* December 16, 1982.
13. "Brazilian Leader at U.N. Foresees Major Depression," *New York Times,* October 28, 1982.
14. IFRI, p. 181.

Chapter 6

1. Term used in the *Wall Street Journal,* May 5, 1982, by writer Tim Metz.
2. "Bankrupt Securities as Growth Issue," *New York Times,* June 13, 1982.
3. "Braniff Situation Raises Questions on Buying Securities in Firms in Bankruptcy Proceedings," *Wall Street Journal,* May 18, 1982.
4. "Investing in Bankruptcies," *Financial World,* January 15, 1980.
5. "Taking a Flier on Braniff and Other Bankrupts Is a Risky Game, Even for Savvy Speculators," *Wall Street Journal,* May 24, 1981.
6. Ibid.
7. "Life After Bankruptcy," *Barron's,* February 8, 1982.
8. Mercury I, Ltd, Prospectus, January 3, 1983, Nassau, Bahamas, p. 1.

9. "New Ways to Play the Interest-Rate Markets," *Business Week,* February 8, 1982.
10. Ibid.
11. "Lawyer Aiding Manville Thrives on Bankruptcies," *New York Times,* August 25, 1982.
12. "The Legal Issues in Manville's Move," *New York Times,* August 27, 1982.
13. "Manville's Robust Bankruptcy," *New York Times,* December 10, 1982.
14. "Bankruptcy Court May Establish Precedent," *Business Insurance,* September 6, 1982, p. 30.
15. "Congratulations You're Bankrupt," *Forbes,* March 15, 1982.

Chapter 7

1. Interview with the author, September 1982.
2. Ibid.
3. Edward I. Altman, "Accounting Implications of Failure Prediction Models," *Journal of Accounting, Auditing, & Finance,* 6, no. 1, Fall 1982.
4. Edward I. Altman and James K. La Fleur, "Managing a Return to Financial Health," *Journal of Business Strategy,* Summer 1981, p.35.

The Z-Score formula is:
$$Z = 1.2X_1 + 1.4X_2 + 3.3X_3 + 0.6X_4 + 1.0X_5$$
X_1 is working capital divided by total assets (the value to a buyer if the company were for sale).
X_2 is retained earnings divided by total assets.
X_3 is earnings before interests and taxes divided by total assets.
X_4 is market value of equity divided by book value of total debt.
X_5 is sales divided by total assets.

Z is the overall index of corporate fiscal health.
Company performance as calculated here provides a numerical measure ranging from -4 to $+8$. A high number indicates strong performance.

5. The perspective of the general community affected by the debtor's bankruptcy and the involvement of the political process in the situation are not discussed here. Suffice it to say that it can significantly affect the labor aspects. For example, unions may have the political clout to help obtain subsidized industrial revenue bonds or other public assistance or to put pressure on the company not to close a facility.
6. "Step by Step Through the Costa Rican Saga," *Euromoney,* August 1982, p. 33.

Chapter 8

1. "The Coming Squeeze in Brazil," *Business Week,* September 27, 1982.
2. "The Year of the Rescheduling," *Euromoney,* August 1982.
3. Lester C. Thurow, "If the Debtors Default," *Newsweek,* February 21, 1983.
4. "Brazilian Leader, at U.N., Foresees Major Depression," *New York Times,* September 28, 1982.
5. Interview with the author, April 1983.
6. "Worry at the World's Banks," *Business Week,* September 6, 1983.
7. French Institute for International Relations (IFRI), *RAMSES 1982: The State of the World Economy,* Ballinger Publishing Company, Cambridge, Mass., 1982, p. 137.
8. Harold Lever, "International Banking's House of Cards," *New York Times,* September 24, 1982.
9. "Nations Agree to Hike IMF Funding by $31.8b," *Boston Globe,* February 12, 1983.
10. "Dettes: le spectre de 1929," *L'Express,* February 25, 1983.
11. Interview with the author, February 15, 1983.
12. "Banks Revise Ways of Making Loans," *Wall Street Journal,* February 18, 1983.
13. "Bankers to Discuss World Debt," *New York Times,* January 10, 1983.
14. Interview with the author, February, 1983.
15. "The Unique Club of Michel Camdessus," *Euromoney,* August 1982.
16. IFRI, p. 127.
17. Lester Thurow, "If the Debtors Default."
18. Jeffrey E. Garten, "A World Banking Peril," *New York Times,* September 9, 1983.
19. Ibid.
20. "Central Bank Pact Urged on Failures," *Washington Post,* September 14, 1982.

Chapter 9

1. Albert Bressand, "Mastering the 'Worldeconomy,'" *Foreign Affairs,* Spring 1983.
2. Ibid.
3. Charles Warren, *Bankruptcy in U.S. History,* Harvard University Press, Cambridge, Mass., 1935.

INDEX

INDEX

Grant, W. T., xiv, xvii, 32–34, 36, 41, 84
Great Southwest Corporation, 31, 89
Group of Ten, 130, 134
GTI Corporation, 95–96
Guthrie, Randolph, 32

Haiti, 142
Harvard School of Business Administration, 34, 75
Heine, Max, 76–78
Heine Securities Corp., 77
Helms, Jesse, 68
Herzog, Heine, Geduld, Inc., 77
Hodges, George A., 126
House Committee on Banking and Currency, 31
Hughes, Helen, 58

IBM, 36
Import-Export Bank, 13
Indonesia, 129
Inflation, xvi, 5, 8, 34, 44
Inflationary index, xvi
Insolvency, 34; defined, 15, 26
Institute of International Finance, The, 131, 135–38
Interest Equalization Tax, 67
Interest rates, 3, 7–8, 13, 69
International Bank for Reconstruction and Development. *See* World Bank
International Development Association (IDA), 133
International Harvester, 36, 38, 77, 91, 95
International Herald Tribune, 129
International Monetary Fund (IMF), xviii, 4, 62, 69–70, 107, 115, 116, 119, 124, 130–32, 147; defined, 130; and exchange rates, 131; lending

capacity, 132, 134; riots, 127; and Third World, 134, 139
International Telegraph & Telephone Corp., 6
Interstate Stores, 85
Investment, short-term, 56
Israel, 13
Itel, 11, 77
I.T.T., 93

Jamaica, 58
Japan, xviii, 12, 67, 134, 142
Jefferson, Thomas, 19, 23
Junk-bonds, 77

Kaufman, Henry, 9
Kennedy, David, 31
Kidder, Peabody & Co., 35–36, 78
Kidder, William M., 78
Kieves, Larry, 49, 52, 56
King Resources Co., 85
Klinck, Mason, 65–66
Korea: South Korea, xiii, xviii, 4, 8, 82, 144; North Korea, 67
Koskinen, John A., 89–91, 93
Kruse, Scott, 87, 97–98

Labor creditors committees, 102
LaFleur, James, 95–96
Latin America, 141–42
Lawyers, corporate bankruptcy, 79–81
Lazard Frères & Company, 50, 64
Lehman Brothers Kuhn Loeb, 64, 103, 108, 128, 139
Lever, Harold, 57, 64
Leverage, 7
Levin, Weintraub & Crames, 79
Levitt & Sons, 93
Lifland, Burton R., 80
Lindsay, John, 46

Pacific Exchange, 77
Palmieri, Victor, 87–94, 129, 145
Pan Am airlines, 95
"Paper" commitment, 40
Pari passu treatment of bonds
    and notes, 110–12, 116–17
Paris Club, The, 138, 146
Pemex, 126–127
Penn Central Co., xv, xvii, 11,
    36, 40, 88–89, 144–45; col-
    lapse, 29–32, 76–77
Penn Central Corp., 32
Penn Central Transportation Co.,
    29, 88
Penn Square Bank, xiv, 9, 39
Pennsylvania Company, 31
Pertamina oil company, 129
Peru, 63, 68, 127, 142
Phoenix Resources Co., 85
Pierce, Fenner & Smith, 54
Pittsburgh, Pennsylvania, 48
Poland, xv, 15; austerity meas-
    ures in, 126; bankruptcy in,
    58; debt of, xiv, 5, 9, 56–63,
    68, 144; default option of, 65;
    economy of, 9, 58, 60–61;
    GNP, 59; insolvency of, xvii;
    Solidarity movement in, 57,
    61, 126; and the Soviet Union,
    57, 68
Pre-petition claims, 100
Prince, Michael F., 78
Profits, short-term, xvii
Proposition 2½, 51
Proposition 13, 51
Puz, Richard, 128

R. L. Burns Corporation, 40
Rangel, Carlos, 141
Recession, xiii, 3, 8, 10, 14
Reagan, Ronald, 51, 132–33,
    142; budget, 12–13, 144; mili-
    tary program, 53
Regan, Donald T., 8, 59, 134

Reich, Robert, 7
Revenue Sharing Act, 52
Rockefeller, Nelson, 45, 50
Rohatyn, Felix, 14, 47–50, 53,
    59, 68, 129, 139, 145
Rolling over (renewing) of debt,
    4, 8
Romania, 5, 58, 62, 126
Rotberg, Gene, 63

S. G. Warburg, 103, 108, 128
Sahlman, William, 6
Sambo's, 11
Sampson, Anthony, 128
Saudi Arabia, 132
Schmidt, Helmut, 57, 60–61
Schultz, Jeff, 77
Scotland, 18
Seafirst Corporation, 10, 127
Sears Roebuck, 36
Securities, short-term, 54
Securities and Exchange Comis-
    sion (SEC), 43, 53, 55, 92, 96,
    145
Shadow Open Market Commit-
    tee, 139
Sherman, Roger, 23
Shuchman, Philip G., 80
Siam, 18
Sigoloff, Sanford C., 37, 91
Simmons, Charles III, 82–83
Simmons Machine Tool, 82
Simonnot, Philippe, 135
Singapore, xiii
Social security system, 13
Southwest and Southeast Pension
    Fund, 93
Soviet Union, 18, 60, 66; banks
    in, 66–67; and Poland, 57, 68;
    and the United States, 68
Sprague, Peter, 81
Standard & Poor rating service,
    48, 54
Stange, Werner, 136–38

160

ABOUT THE AUTHOR

Dan Dimancescu is a business consultant and writer. In recent years his work has concentrated on comparisons of national policies to promote high technology industries. His analysis focuses primarily on the electronics and computer industry. In 1982, he was the co-author with James Botkin and Ray Stata of *Global Stakes: The Future of High Technology in America.* This book received wide national attention and helped stimulate a major legislative initiative to create a sustained matching funds mechanism for engineering and science education in the United States.

Dimancescu studied at Dartmouth College, the Fletcher School of Law and Diplomacy, and the Harvard School of Business Administration. He has lectured at the Kennedy Institute of Politics at Harvard University. He is currently a partner with the Technology and Strategy Group in Cambridge, Massachusetts, and a founder of Interex Associates with offices in Lincoln, Massachusetts.

ACKNOWLEDGMENTS

This manuscript was written on a Wang word processor. Outside of the assumed advantages, one benefit was to allow completion of the text without secretarial help. While the resulting savings in cost are significant, they are equaled by an immense saving in time. Numerous chapter revisions were completed during the twelve months required to complete the text. A "clean" revised chapter could be re-typed in five to ten minutes; a full text of the book could be produced in less than an hour. Within nine days of delivering edited floppy disks to the typesetter full galleys were returned for final proofing.

The glitter of new technololgy is meaningless, however, without countless hours of human effort. Quality in a text comes in large part from the final polishing of thoughts and words by editors. For this I am very thankful to Steven Cramer, Julie Doohan and to Cheryl Brooks who also created the index.

Jacket design and page layouts are by the author. The type chosen is Times Roman. Typesetting and page make-up are by Jay's Publishers Services, Inc., in Rockland, Massachusetts.

Since the early 1970s, the crisis of debt has grown to such proportions that it threatens the stability of Western economies.

In a fast-paced, engaging book for both layman and specialist, Dan Dimancescu explores three facets of spiraling debt obligations in the United States and the world. Starting with the infamous collapse of Penn Central in 1970, he explains the new phenomenon of bankruptcy that is reaching into America's largest corporations. He discusses the shocking financial crisis of New York City as an example of local government debt in the United States. Finally, the growing magnitude of international debt is revealed in a discussion of Poland's default to Western banks during the 1970s and the even larger crisis in Brazil and Mexico during the early 1980s.

Have these crises led to a new business of debt and bankruptcy? The author provides compelling insights into the ways debt and bankruptcy have acquired a business life of their own, reveals how they have become a very profitable new Wall Street activity, and outlines some thought-provoking remedies to the current financial crisis.

One outcome of what he terms "the financiers' decade" is a new breed of managers. With skills acquired turning around and managing the